Sculpting a Coyote in Soapstone

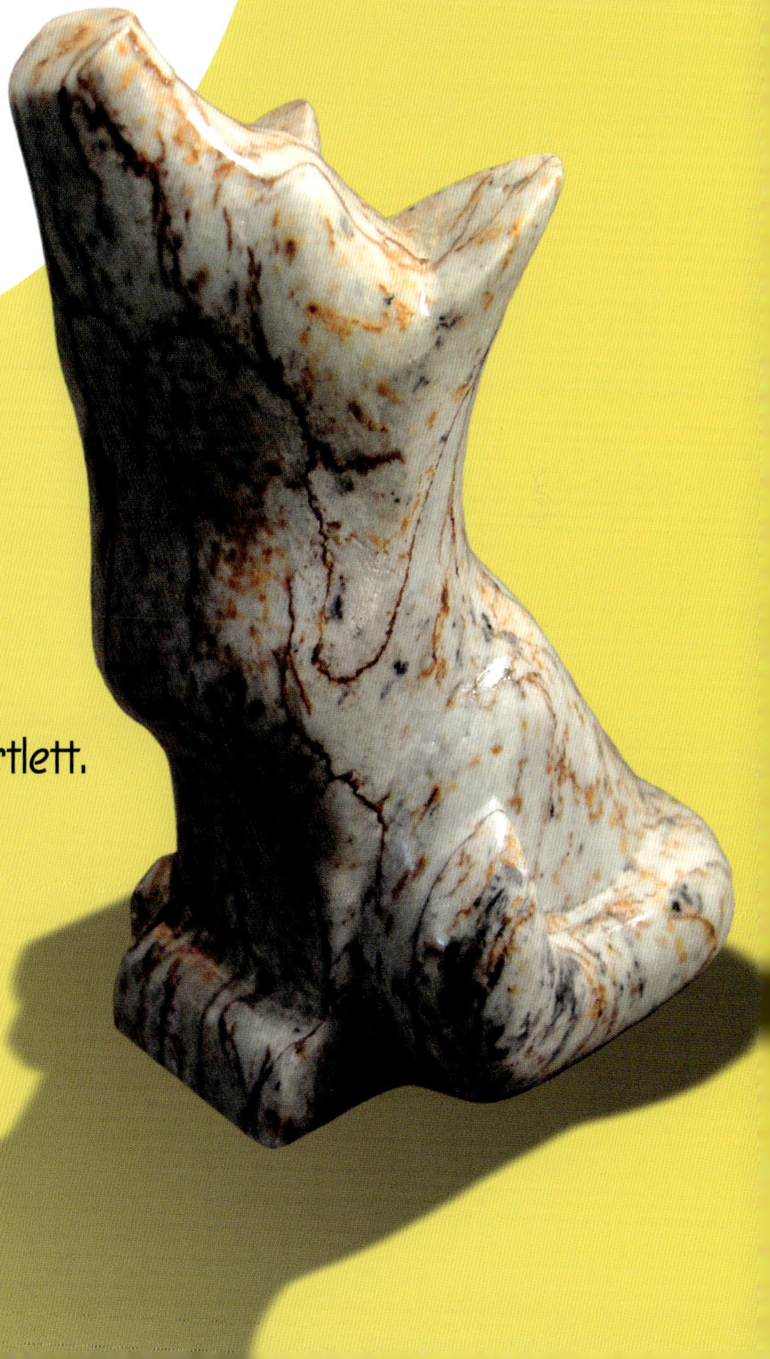

Tasha Unninayar and Lynn Bartlett.
Artist, Dawn Hartwig

Schiffer Publishing Ltd
4880 Lower Valley Road · Atglen, Pennsylvania 19310

Other Schiffer Books By The Author:
Introduction to Soapstone Sculpting. ISBN: 9780764337819. $29.99

Other Schiffer Books on Related Subjects:
Carving in Soap. Howard K. Suzuki. ISBN: 0764312928. $12.95

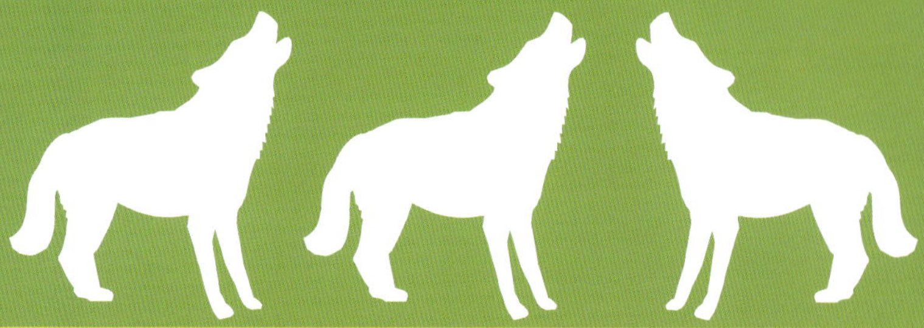

Schiffer Books are available at special discounts for bulk purchases for sales promotions or premiums. Special editions, including personalized covers, corporate imprints, and excerpts can be created in large quantities for special needs. For more information contact the publisher:

Published by Schiffer Publishing Ltd.
4880 Lower Valley Road
Atglen, PA 19310
Phone: (610) 593-1777; Fax: (610) 593-2002
E-mail: Info@schifferbooks.com

For the largest selection of fine reference books on this and related subjects, please visit our website at
www.schifferbooks.com
We are always looking for people to write books on new and related subjects. If you have an idea for a book, please contact us at
proposals@schifferbooks.com

This book may be purchased from the publisher.
Include $5.00 for shipping.
Please try your bookstore first.
You may write for a free catalog.

In Europe, Schiffer books are distributed by
Bushwood Books
6 Marksbury Ave.
Kew Gardens
Surrey TW9 4JF England
Phone: 44 (0) 20 8392 8585; Fax: 44 (0) 20 8392 9876
E-mail: info@bushwoodbooks.co.uk
Website: www.bushwoodbooks.co.uk

Library of Congress Control Number: 2011942467

Designed by RoS
Type set in SquireD/Humanist 521 BT

ISBN: 978-0-7643-4009-3
Printed in China

Dedication

This book is dedicated to a dear friend and amazing person, Phil Arnott. Thank you Phil for helping us to get to the other side. It would not have been possible without you.

Acknowledgments

We would like to first thank our publisher for the opportunity to share the art of soapstone carving in another great book and also thanks to Hobby Lobby for supplying the materials and supplies.

For this project, *Sculpting a Coyote in Soapstone,* Lynn and I selected a very talented sculptor as our featured artist: Dawn Hartwig. Her years of experience and talent show in even the most basic of projects and we are just thrilled to share with you her techniques and approach. Thank you Dawn for working with us and for the great chats during our sessions. It was a lot of fun getting to know you (over our many cups of coffee) and we look forward to more projects—especially an equine one!

Thank you Josh for your encouragement and sense of humor, and Hadean and Seidon for being just the most wonderful things in the world.

We would both like to thank our dear friends and family who have encouraged us through this process. We hope that you will find as much inspiration in carving the playful coyote as we have. Happy Carving!

Authors
Tasha Unninayar and Lynn Bartlett

Contents

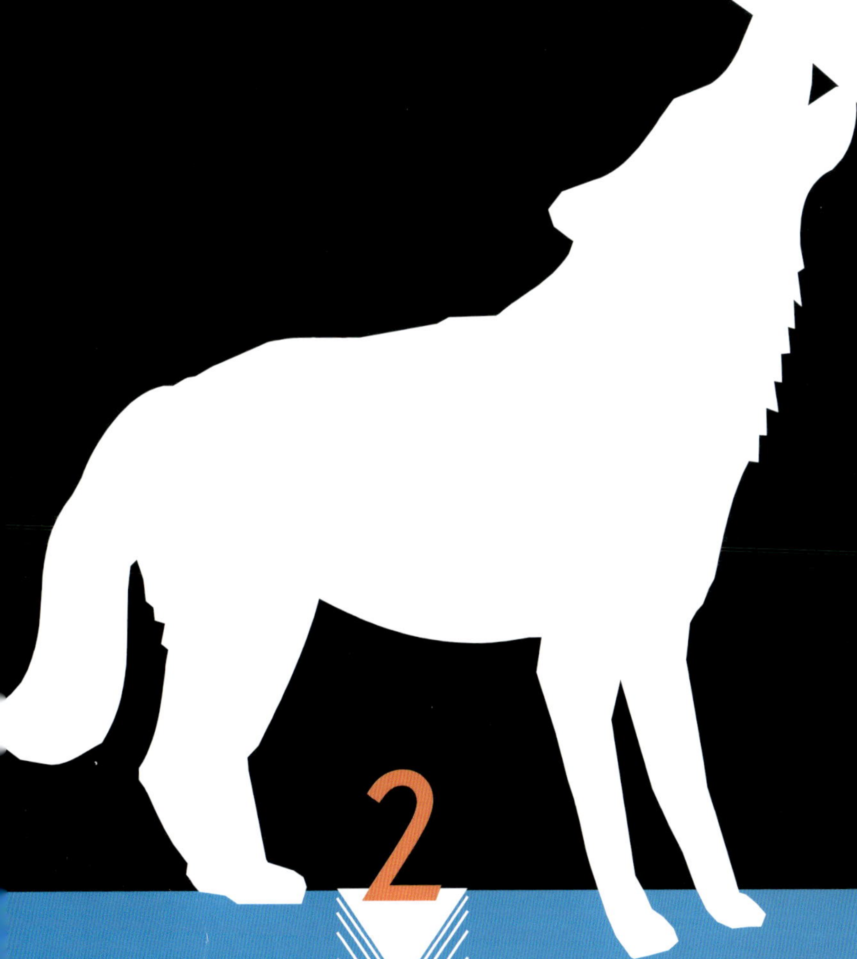

2

3

Carving the Coyote

Finishing and Polishing

A Brief Introduction to Soapstone

There are many materials available for sculptors to create with, such as wood, clay, marble, alabaster, and soapstone. Soapstone has always been a favorite material because of its softness and ease to sculpt and manipulate. New sculptors of any age and skill level can easily accomplish fun projects with soapstone. This positive reinforcement encourages them to continue creating and learning this craft. The art of carving stone gives you the special feeling that you are creating something that will last forever, and may even be a part of history. Your piece may become a family heirloom.

There are many techniques that you can learn, ranging from the use of electric tools, found at your local hardware store, to ancient techniques that have been passed down for generations. The best part is that you don't need much to complete your coyote. You can create it at home, in the garage, in a classroom or any comfortable space of your choosing.

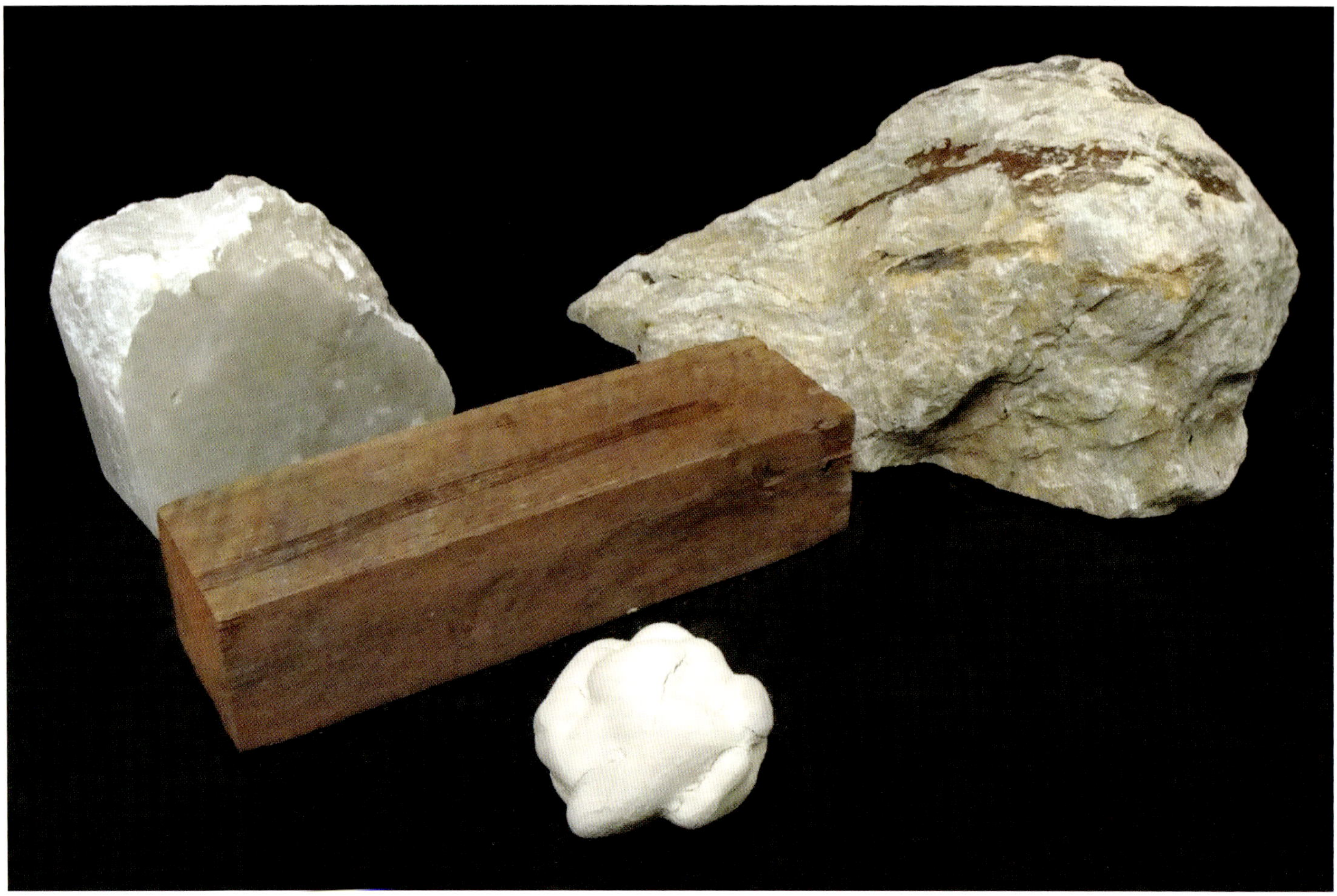

White marble in raw form, wood block, golden soapstone in raw form and clay.

History of the Coyote

For generations and in many cultures the coyote has been seen as the playful prankster, having insight and wisdom. Perhaps that is why we cannot help but feel a little whimsy when we look at a coyote. The coyote symbolizes duality and the ability to present both sides of an issue. He is also full of humor and is a little sarcastic. The coyote has been a popular subject across many media.

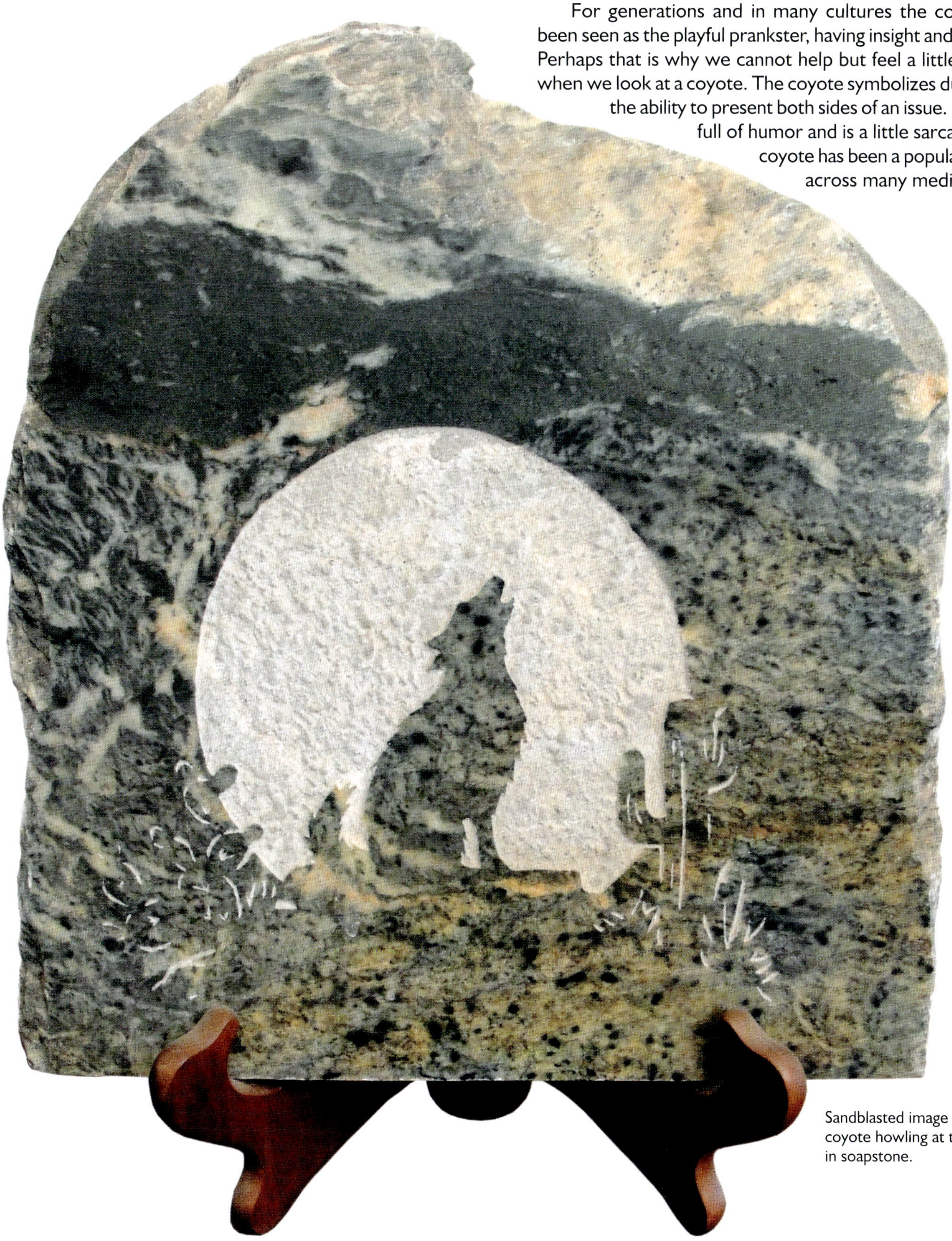

Sandblasted image of a coyote howling at the moon, in soapstone.

Preparing Your Space

Hopefully you are lucky enough to be able to work out of doors on your projects, making the debris easy to clean up. If this is the case, find a table that you can work on (one that you do not strain your back using). Using lots of newspaper, cover your table in layers that you can remove as dust accumulates. If you put a wet towel under your soapstone project, you can trap the dust that collects and discard it as you go by rinsing out the towel. You can create a "sandbag" out of an old pair of blue jeans. Cut a leg into a section and stitch one end. Fill the leg with silica sand (do not overstuff the leg), stitch the other end, and *bingo* you have a wonderful place to work your stone.

If you are forced to work indoors, you can use a kitty litter box or small box and fill it half way with silica sand (purchased at the hardware store—they refer to it as Play Sand). This box will now act as both a cushion for the piece to be worked in and a dust collector.

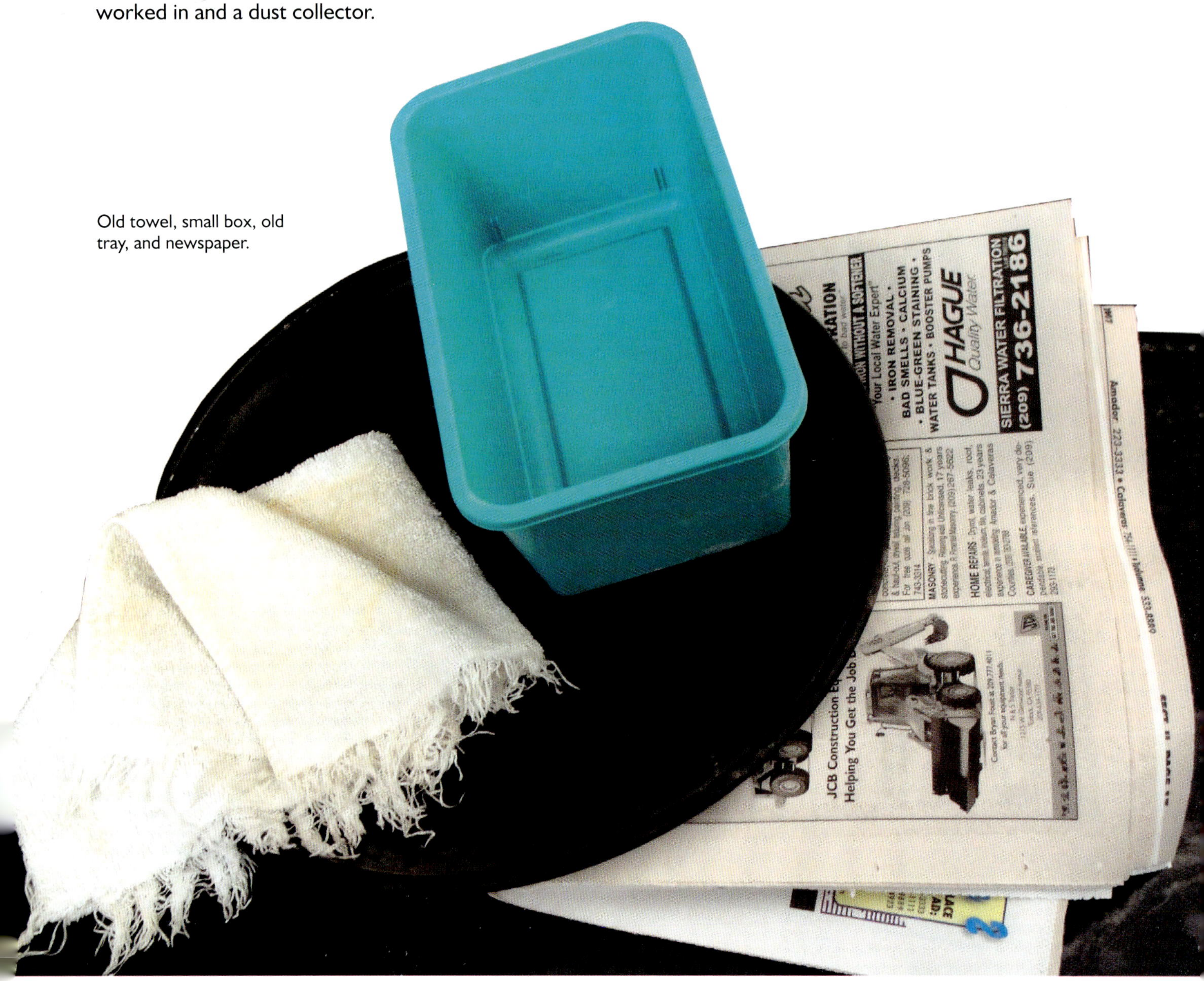

Old towel, small box, old tray, and newspaper.

Supplies You Will Need

For your coyote you will need a piece of soapstone, in this case we used a precut stone of the coyote design (you can purchase the stone precut at most suppliers or request your supplier to cut it to this size and/or cut it yourself). You can also use a raw piece of stone or a block of stone that you cut down to the basic shape. In this project we used a rasp, a four-sided file, and a flat chisel. However, the project can be accomplished with a mere rasp, but this process would take quite a bit more time and effort. You will also need a pencil, sandpaper (beginning with 80 grit, 120 grit, and 220 grit), steel wool, and some olive oil, or spray lacquer, for the finish. Optional supplies are a plastic mat to set the piece on, a plastic box, newspaper or old towel to catch the debris from the filing.

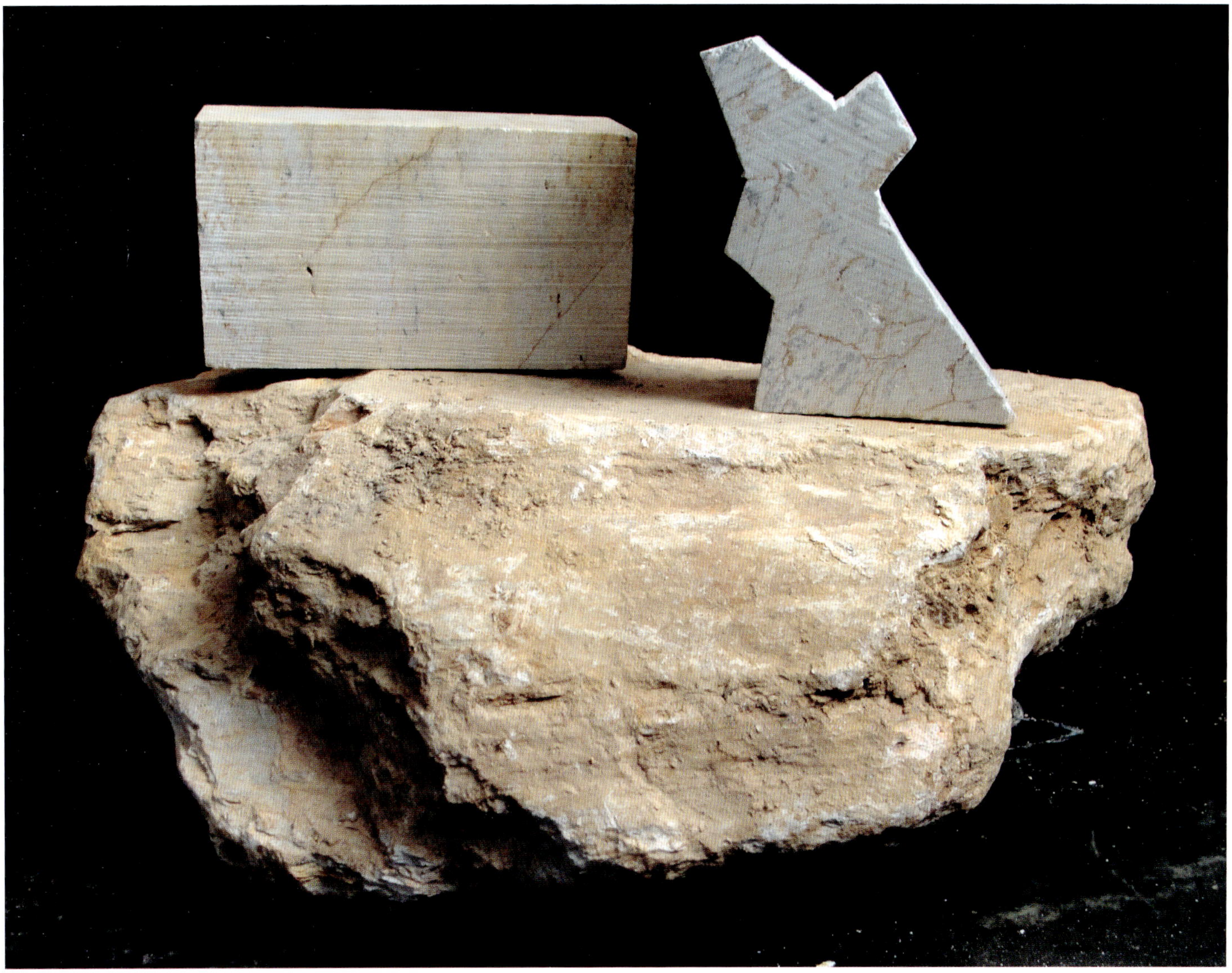

Raw soapstone, blocked stone, and a precut coyote design.

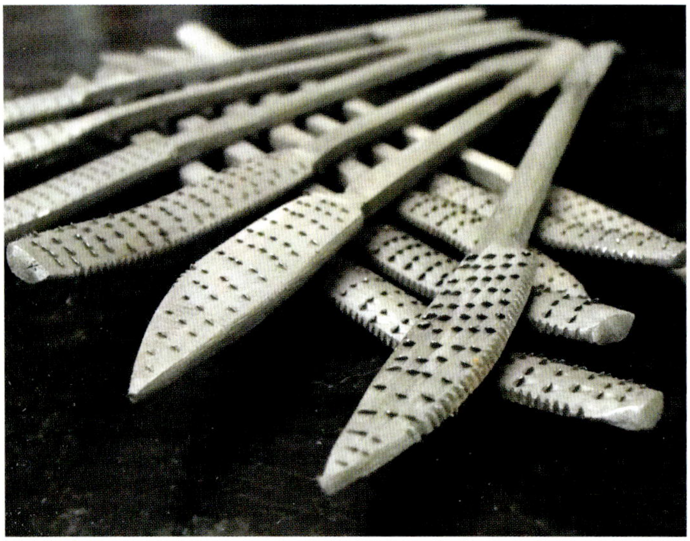

Rasps

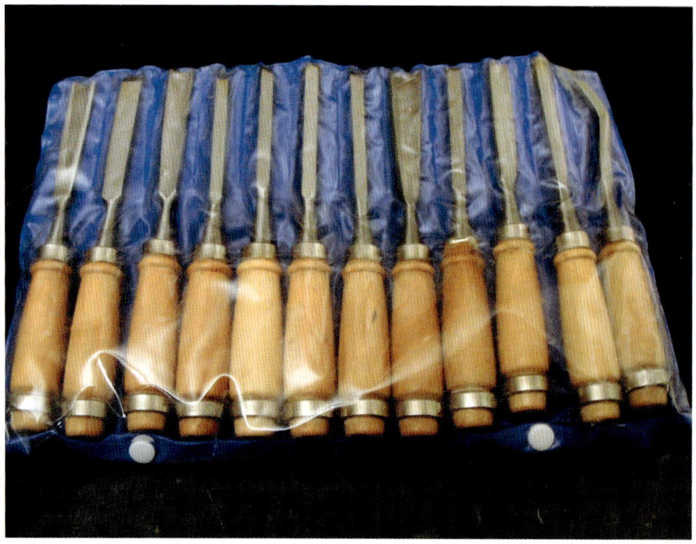

An example of a chisel set, but you can use any type of flat chisel.

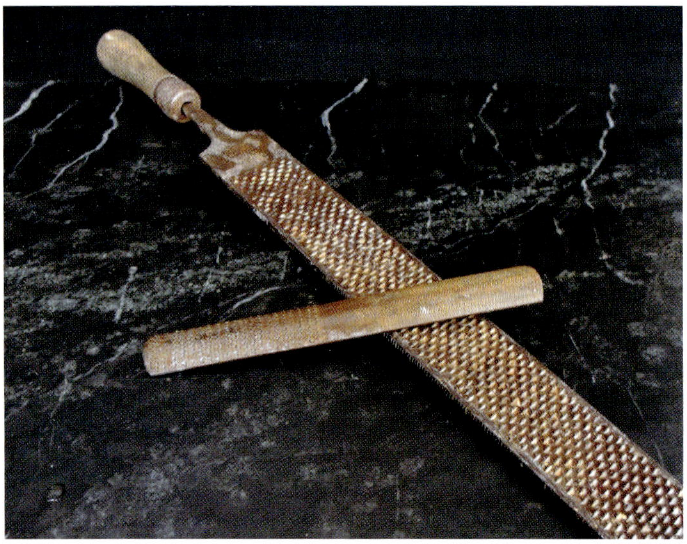

Flat four-sided files, large and small. In this project we used the small file.

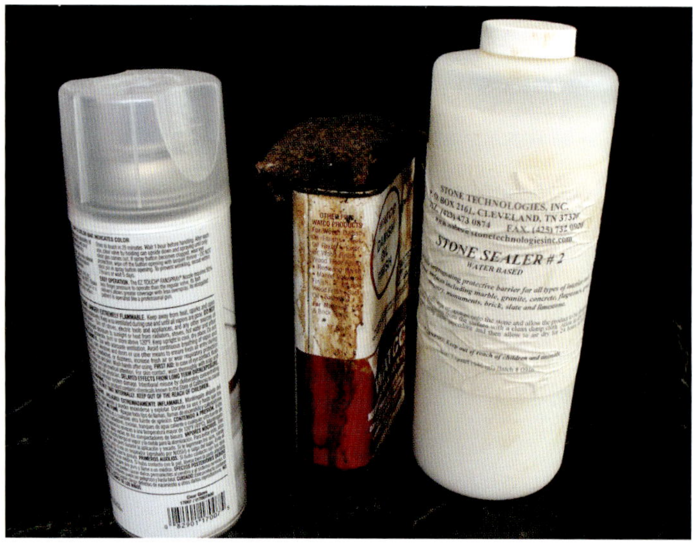

Spray lacquer, sealer, and polish.

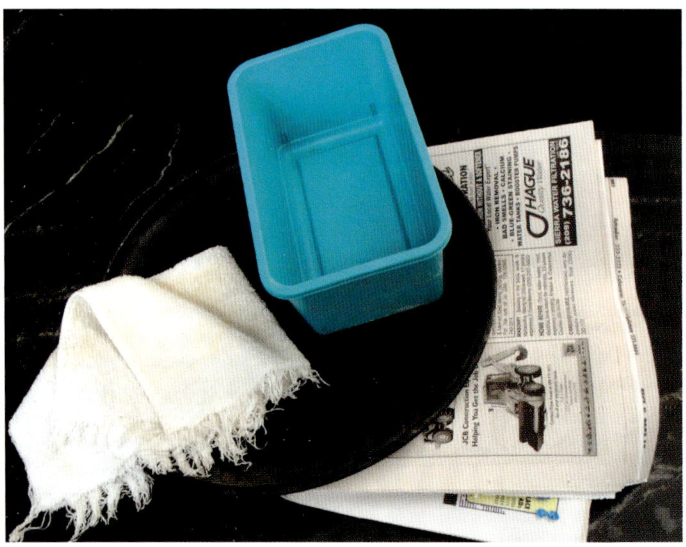

Small box, old towel, old tray, and newspaper.

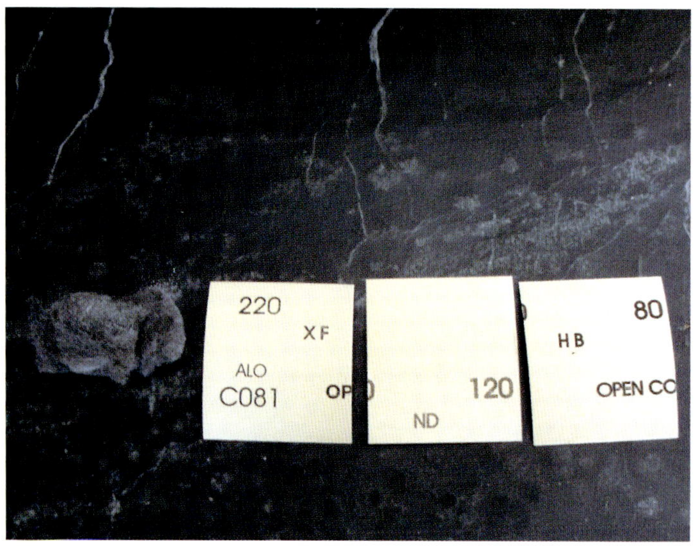

80, 120, and 220 grit sandpaper, along with 0000 steel wool.

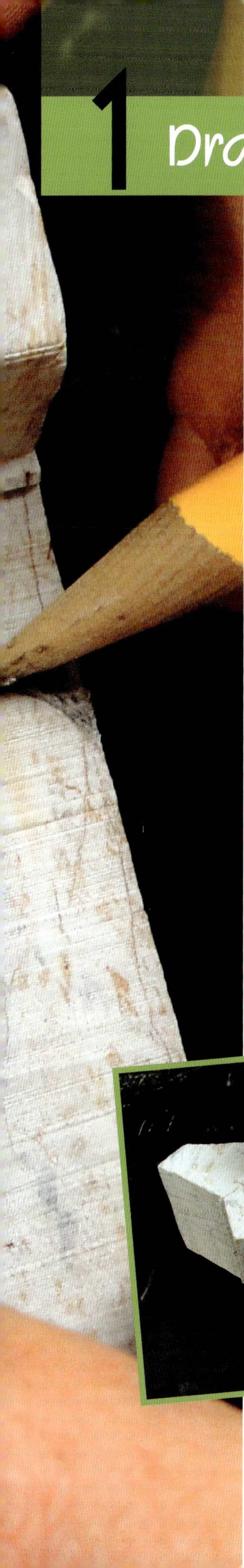

1 Drawing the Design

You can use the project pattern or draw the design freehand. In this case we drew the design freehand on the stone. At any time during the creation of your sculpture, we encourage you to look ahead at the photos so that you can visualize the process before you execute any of the steps.

Take your precut piece of soapstone and place it in your hands so that the head and nose are facing to the left. Pick up your pencil and begin drawing the design.

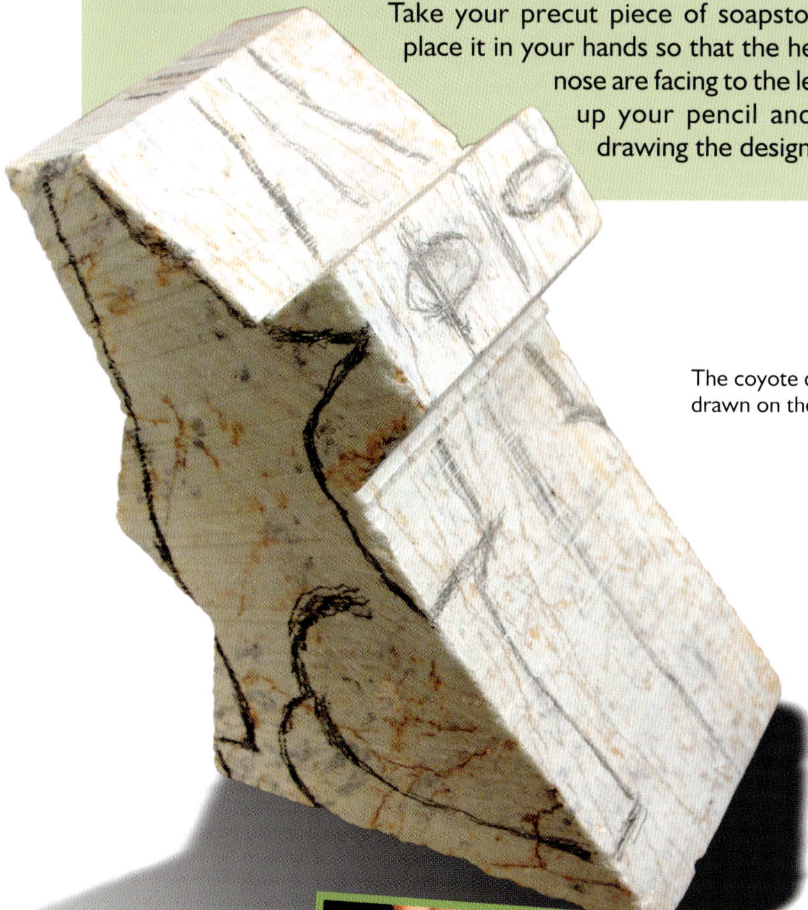

The coyote design drawn on the block.

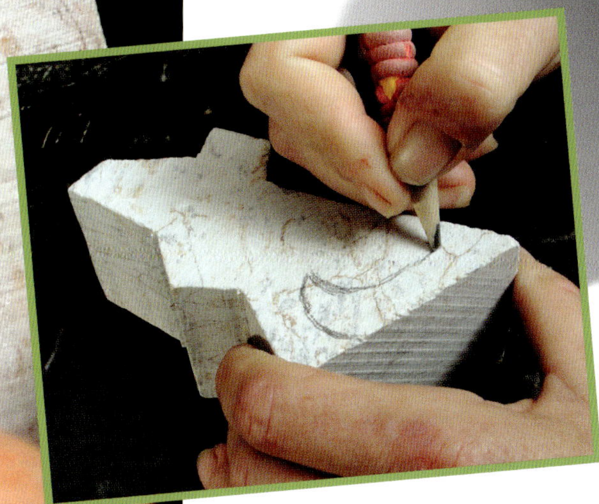

Begin drawing the tip of the tail, leaving enough room for the front paws. Draw the tip of the tail nice and thick. Continue the line to the edge of the stone.

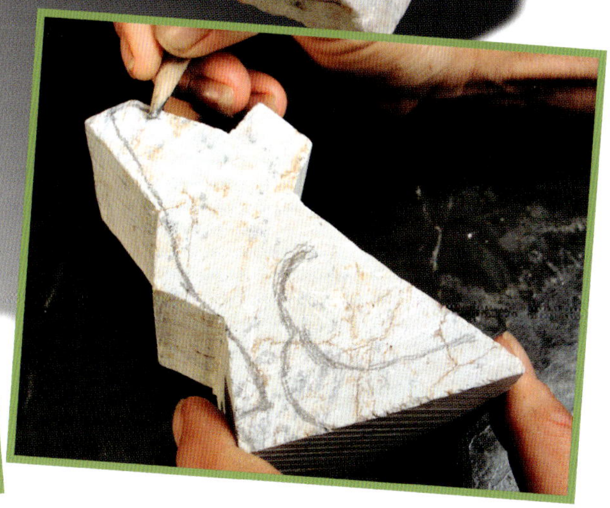

Draw in the curve for the leg behind the tail. Begin drawing the curve of the front legs, starting with the base of the paws. Go straight up the leg. Bring the curve to a point for the chest. Curve back in a little to meet the neck as the head points up. Continue up the jaw. And finally to meet the top of the nose, at the top of the stone. Draw in the flat part of the nose and begin going down the muzzle.

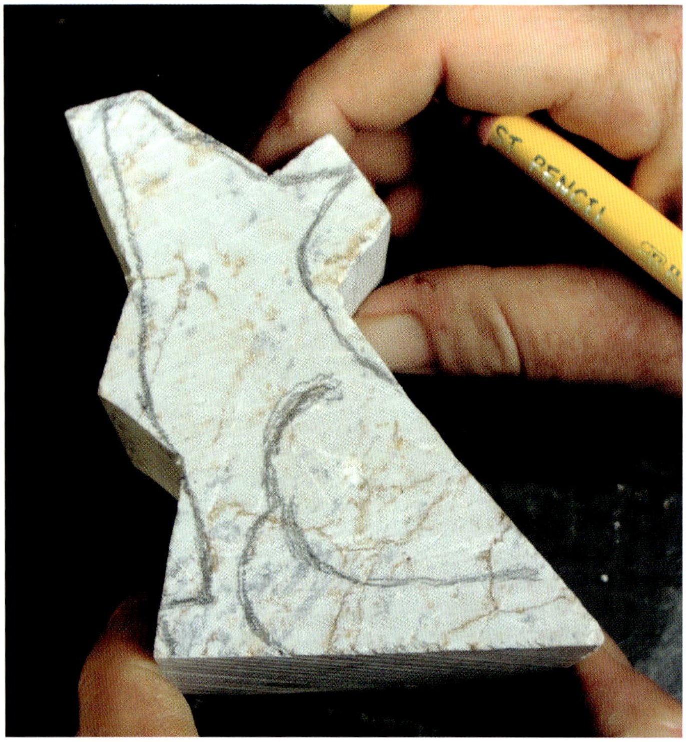

Be sure to leave a little indentation before the eyebrow. Continue around to the ear. Make the ears nice and pointy. Follow the line back down the piece just off the stone's edge. You now have the design drawn in on one side.

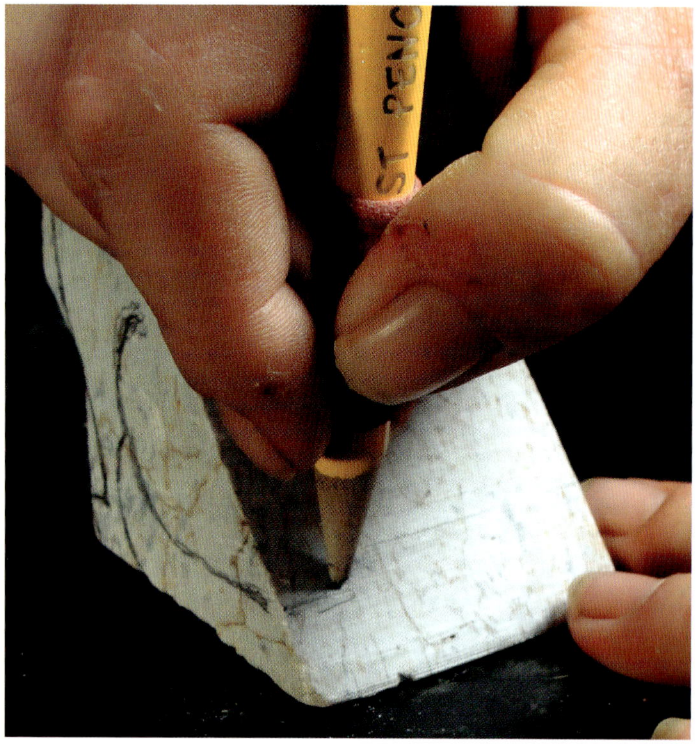

Place your piece standing up and continue the line from the tail onto the back side.

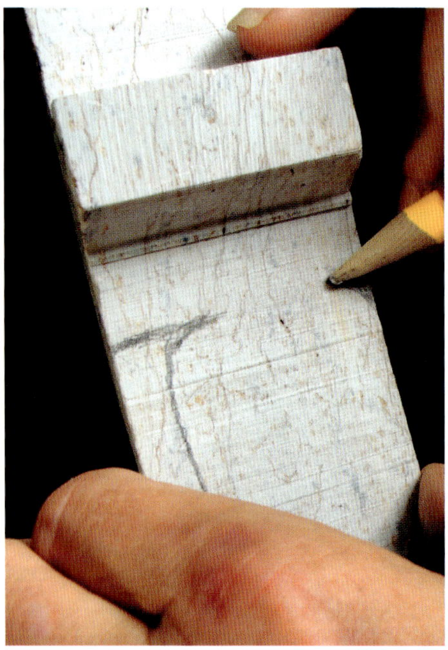

Then continue the line of the top shoulder onto the backside. The lines should be about 1/2" in from the side or so, to allow for the thickness of the tail. Draw in the line connecting the two for the body. Mirror the shoulder line on the other side.

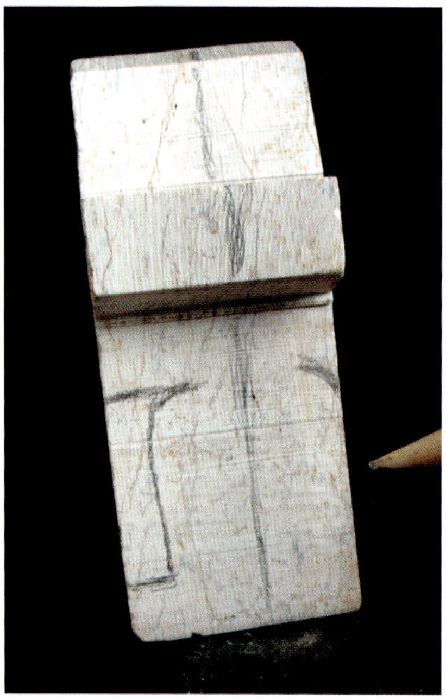

Find the center of the body, not the center of the stone. Remember your body is off center to allow for the tail. Continue the centerline up the piece of the stone and over the head area. The centerline always helps to keep your symmetry.

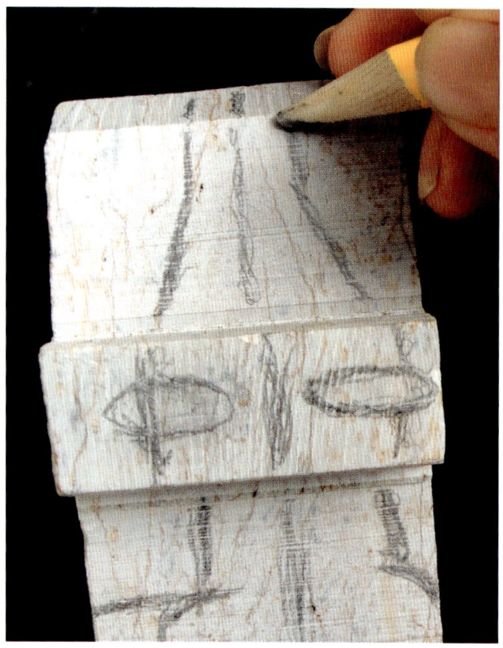

Now put in the lines for the small portion of the body and shoulders. Turn your piece slightly sideways so you can see the tips of the ears and draw in the ears. We draw in ovals at the ear placement to allow for the material at the base of the ear. Draw in the line for the jaw and head. Follow it to the top of the piece to reach the tip of the nose. Repeat on the other side. Continue the line up to the top.

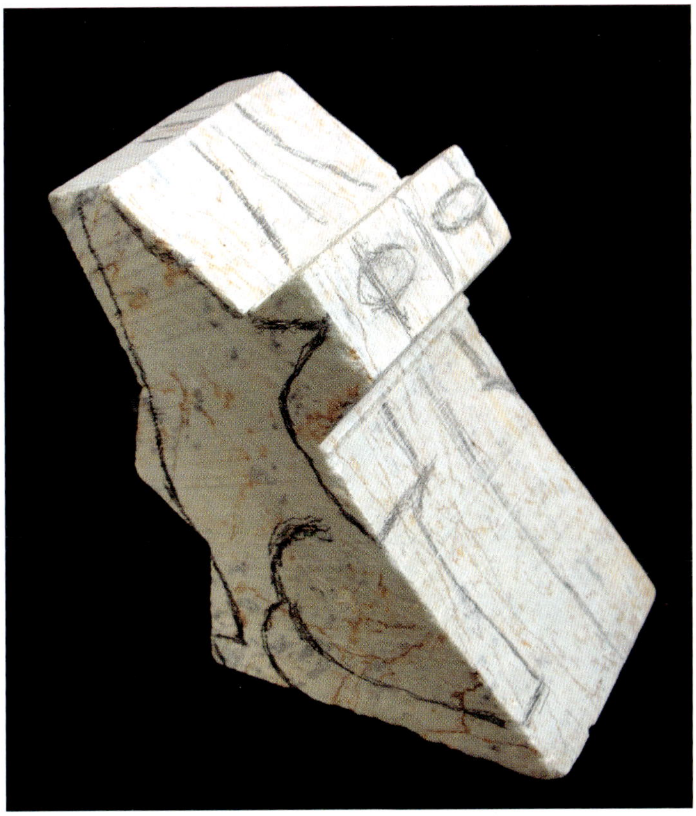

Don't forget to go over the flat tip part. Your piece should look something like this.

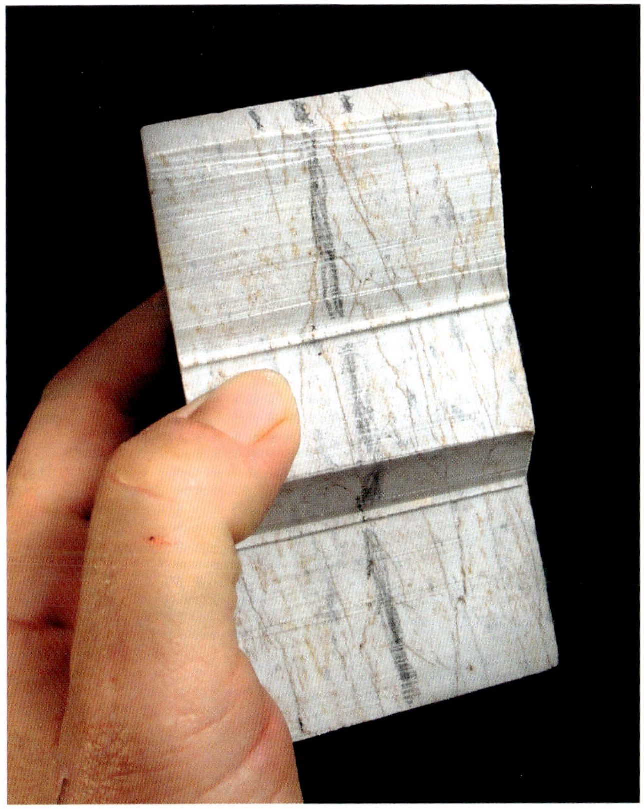

Now angle it so that you see the left side and the front. Take the centerline down the front. Continue past the chest and all the way to the bottom.

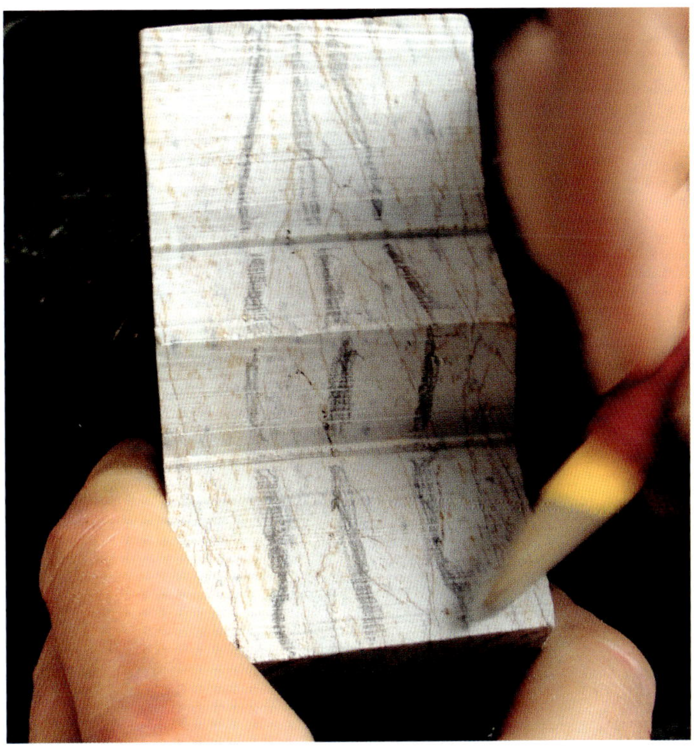

At the top, start drawing in the lines for the head. From this view, the lines almost go straight down. With some light curves. Repeat on the other side. Continue your lines down to the bottom of the stone. Remember these lines are guidelines and you will have a chance to adjust them if needed. The lines do not need to be perfect at this stage.

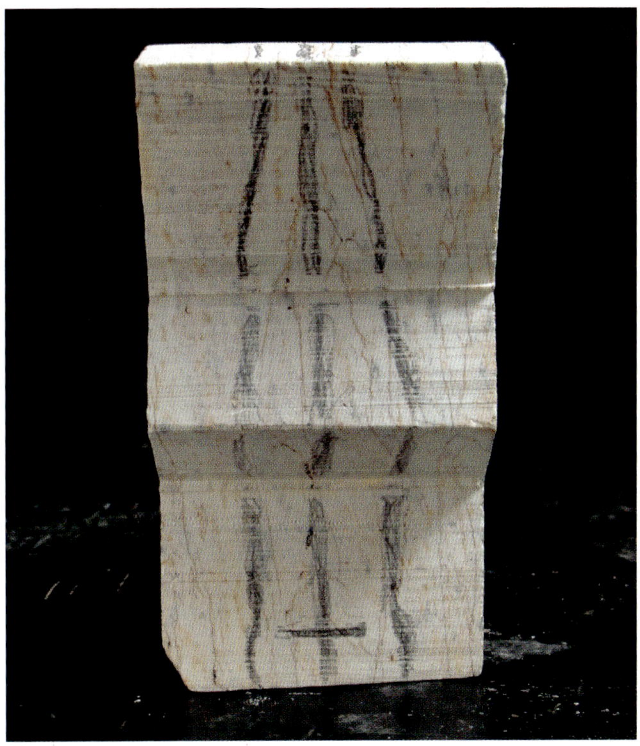

Put in the line for the top of the paws. Now your design is drawn and we can begin the next step.

2 Carving the Coyote

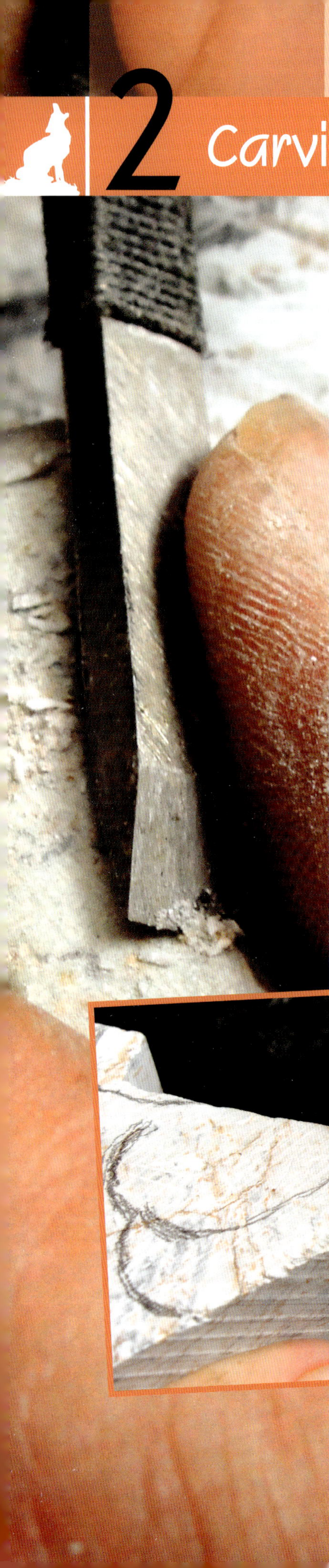

Here you will be using a flat chisel to remove material around the tail and prepare the area on the left side. If you do not have a flat chisel, you can use any type of rasp. The chisel, however, is recommended.

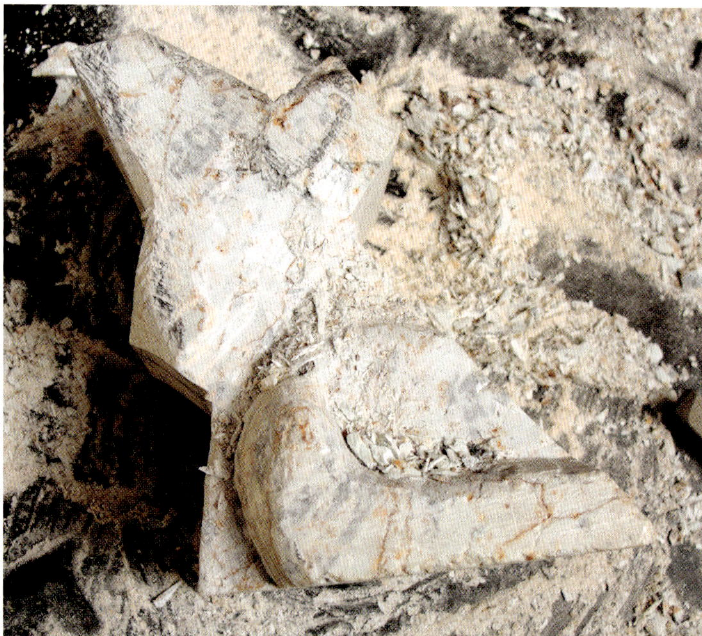

Coyote, tail side.

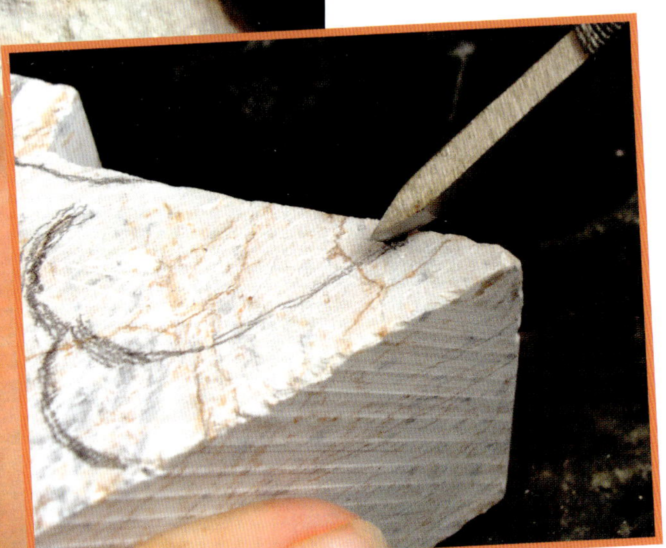

Begin by placing your piece flat with the tail side up. Take your chisel and begin by digging in a corner at the edge of the piece on the tail line.

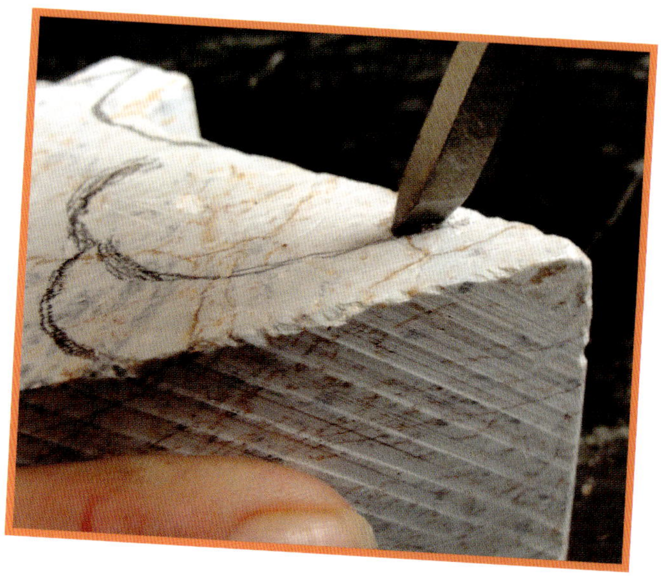

Then rock the chisel with a little pressure to a flat position along the line.

Preparing the Tail

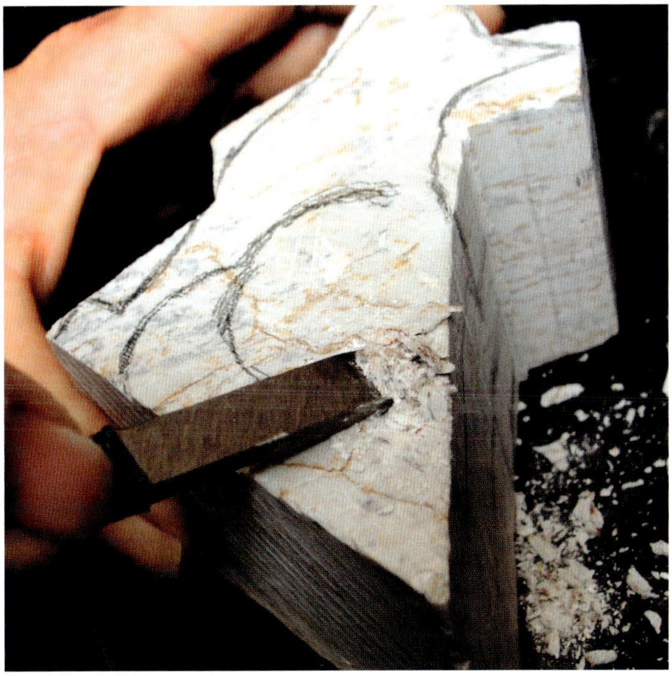

Make sure you have a secure grip on the stone with your left hand (in this case). Apply pressure in a slight upward and away motion from your body on the chisel. This technique allows you to remove material gently while maintaining a line. Practice until you feel more comfortable. Be sure to go slow as to not remove too much material.

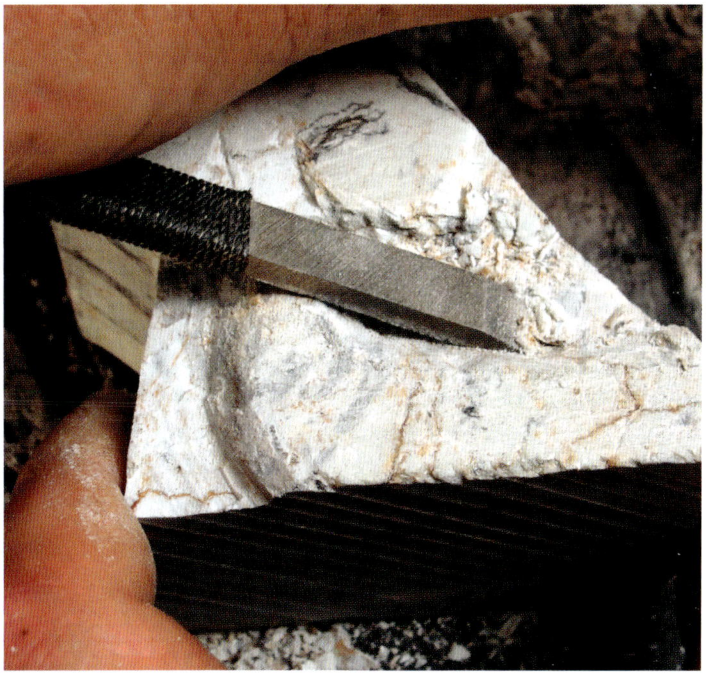

Be sure to be careful as you go around the tip of the tail. You will repeat this motion along the tail several times until you reach the desired depth. Now that you have gone around the tail and have a bit more material removed, you can use the chisel in a flat scrapping motion to evenly "sweep" off material.

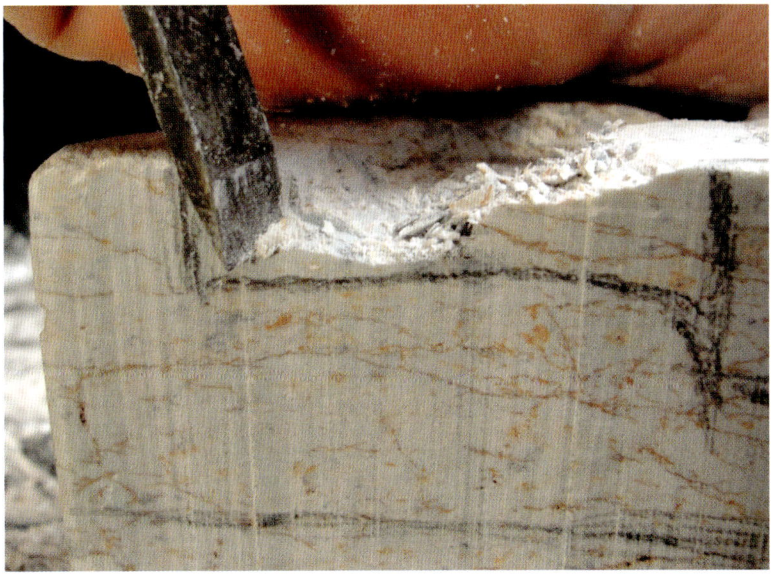

Be careful not cut into the tail. Be sure to expand the area around the tail. If you look at the piece from the side, you will see the lines that you drew. Continue to remove material towards the lines. When you get to the line, stand the chisel up and apply downward pressure. Be especially careful not to go too far. Stop just a little before hitting the line to be on the safe side.

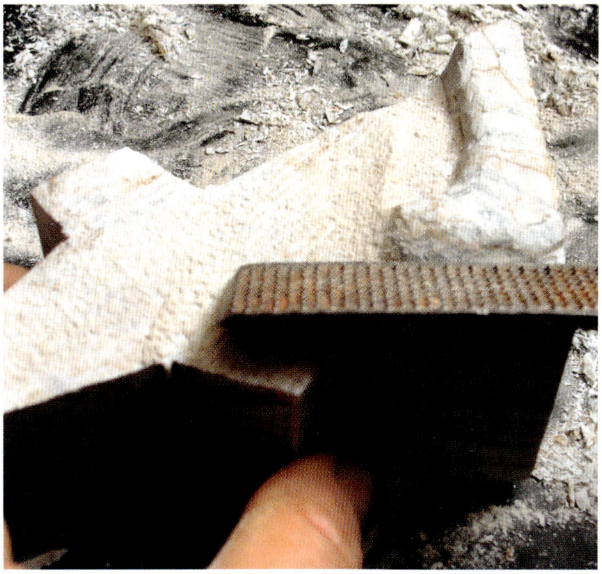

An alternative way to remove material is to use a flat file with a coarse edge. This is a little more aggressive and should be handled carefully around the tip. It is quite effective in removing the material around the whole piece to bring it down to the level of the body.

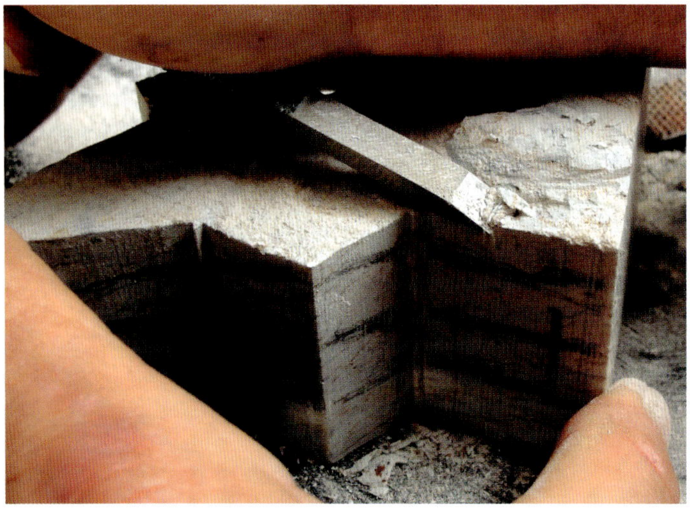

Once we have the material on the body leveled we go back to our flat chisel to continue. Here we are using a slightly different technique by tilting the chisel at an angle against the corner of the stone.

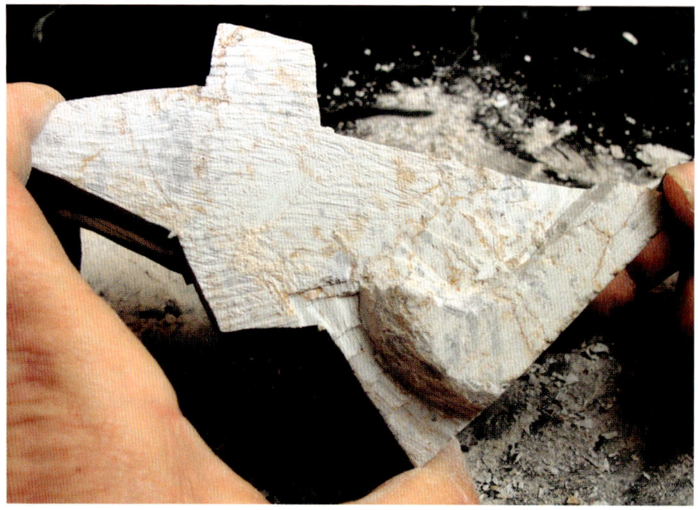

Play around with different chisel positions to see how the material gets removed. Continue removing material a little above the tail. You should have a well defined tail area that stands out from the body. It is always good to take a step back and look at your progress.

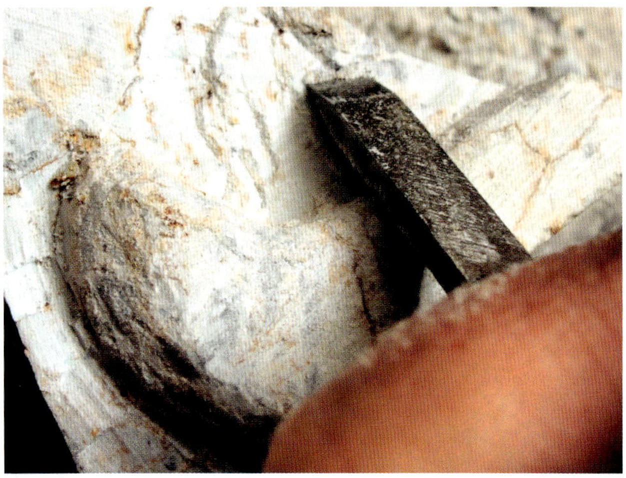

Continue working the area around the tail a bit to smooth out the chisel marks.

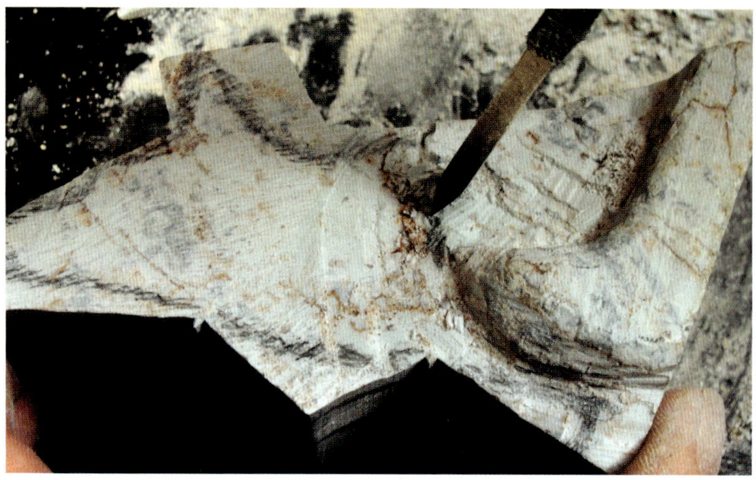

Now, to give your hands a little rest and look at the piece as a whole, get your pencil and draw back in the line for the leg. Also draw the line for the paw and make any lines darker if needed. Draw in the chest line and extend the line up to the top of the stone along the jaw. Follow the bridge of the nose and forehead and continue around the ears down to the leg. Once the lines are drawn in, pick up the chisel again and define the leg.

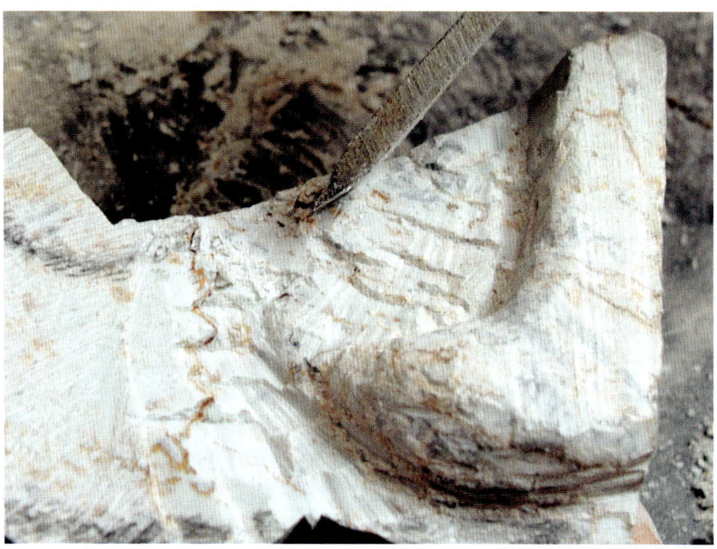

On the edge of the piece, make an indentation for the dip in the lower shoulder and upper leg.

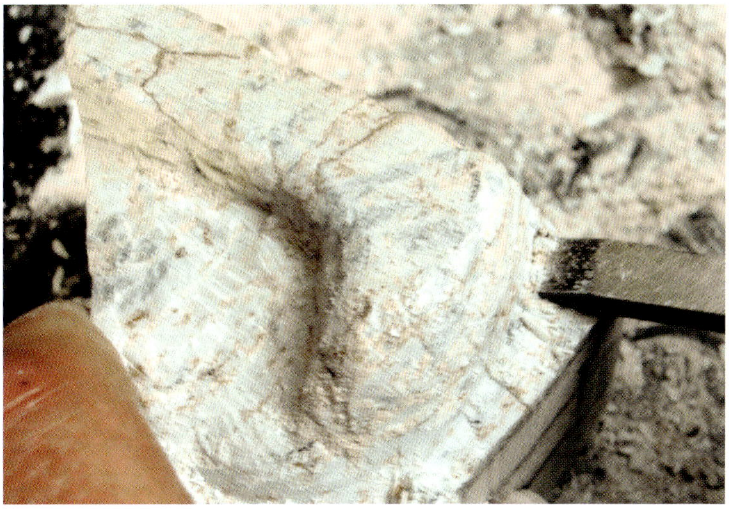

Now take a break from the back and flip the piece over. You will focus on the area below the tail. This technique uses the chisel in a twisting motion. Begin with the chisel pushing down.

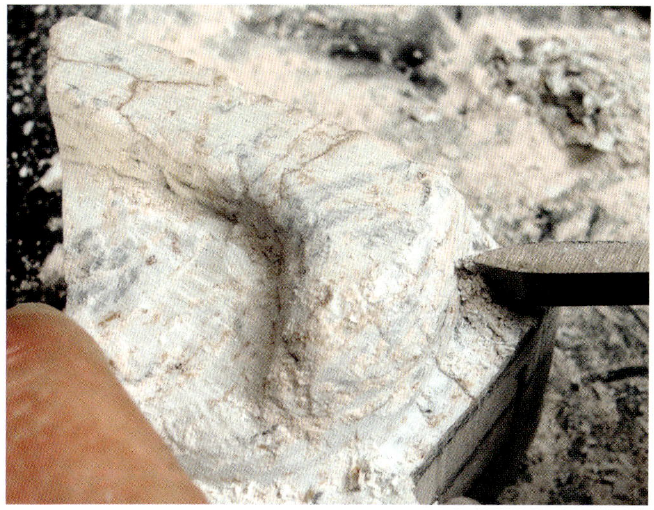

Once the chisel catches some stone, twist the chisel up towards the left, in a counterclockwise motion. Continue this motion up the tail on this side. But do not go around to the top of the tail.

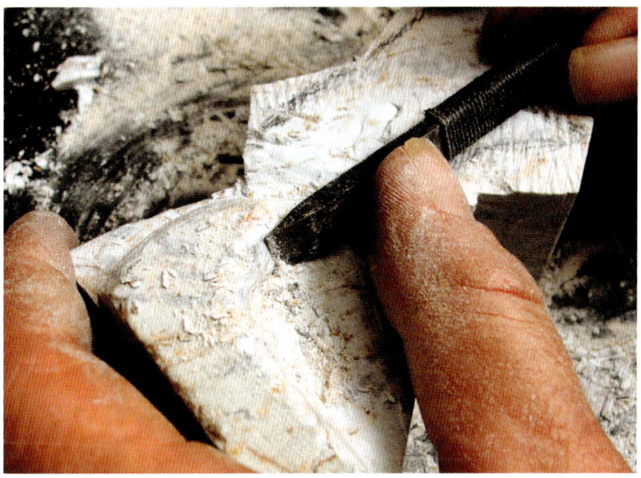

The technique used for the top of the tail is a sweeping, smoothing technique. Take the chisel in an upright position, at an angle, using your thumb for counter pressure and stability. When your grip feels secure, begin contouring the top of the tail with the chisel.

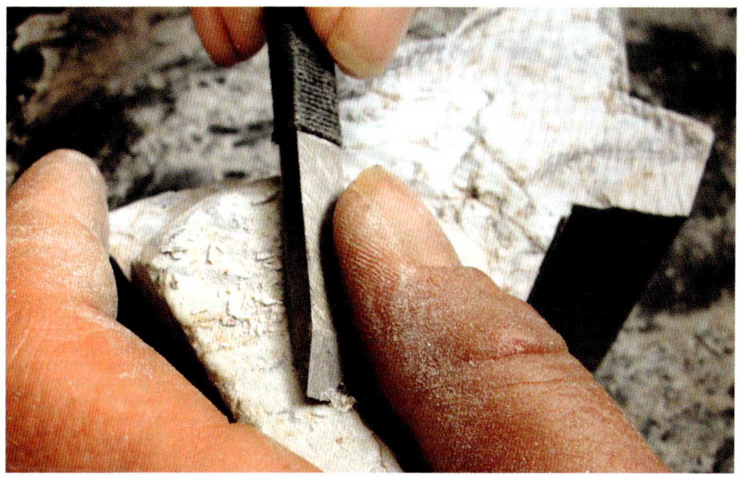

The right hand moves to the left, while the left thumb applies pressure on the chisel against the stone. These are micro movements so as not to dig too deep.

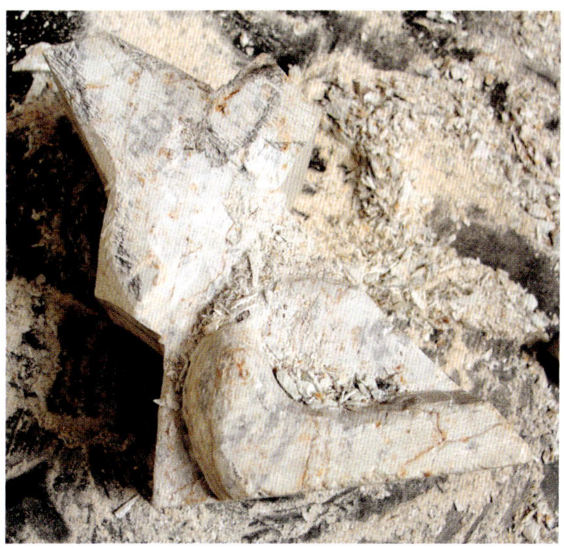

Now that the top of the tail has been defined, go back to the top of the leg and remove a little more material to match the tail depth. Your piece should look something like this. The tail is well defined and the top of the leg area is apparent.

Rounding the Tail Side

Here you will primarily be rounding the tail side of the coyote and enhancing some lines.

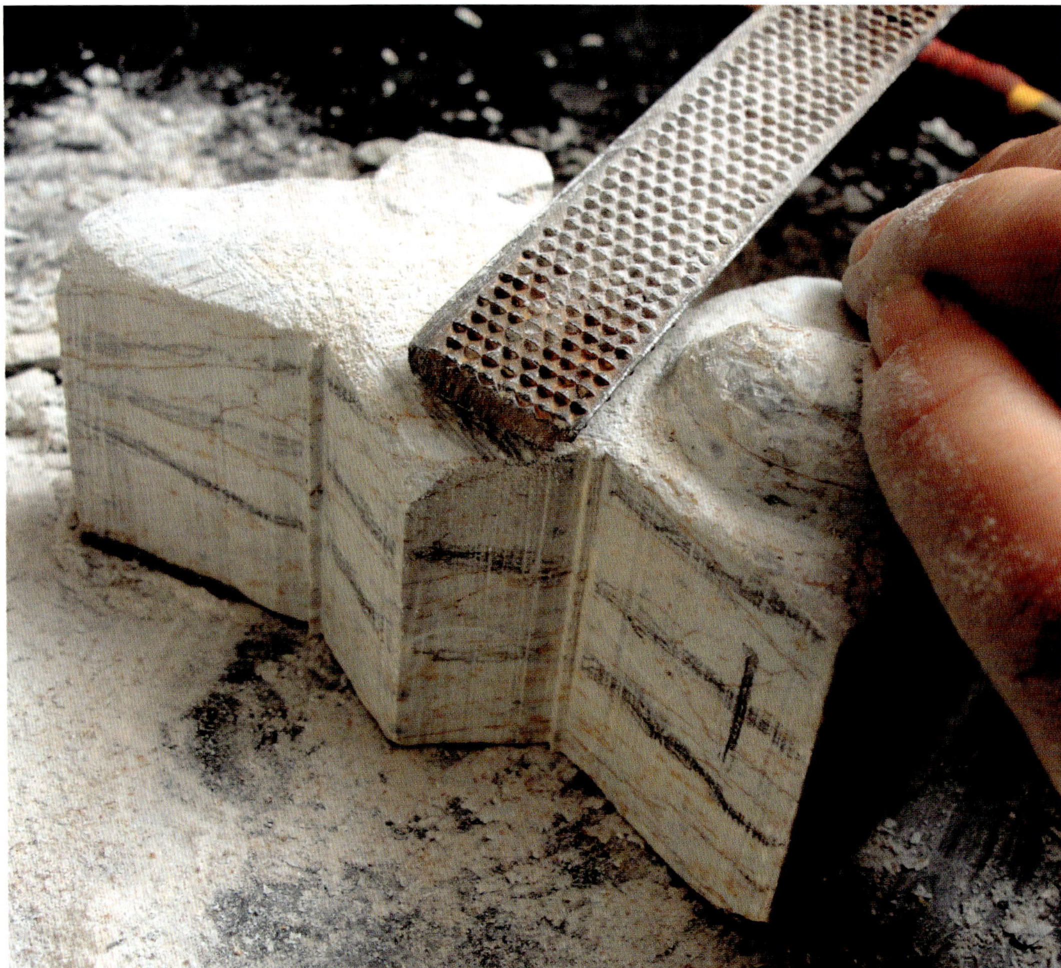

Rounding the tail of the coyote.

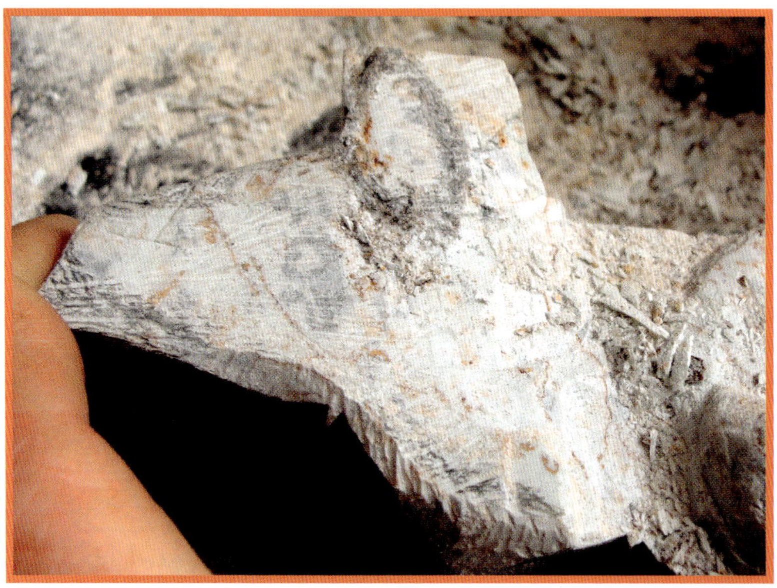

Before getting the file, take your pencil and redefine the ear.
Once the ear is defined in pencil, pick up the flat chisel and notch out the lines. Don't remove too much material around the ear, just enough depth and width to identify the ear placement.

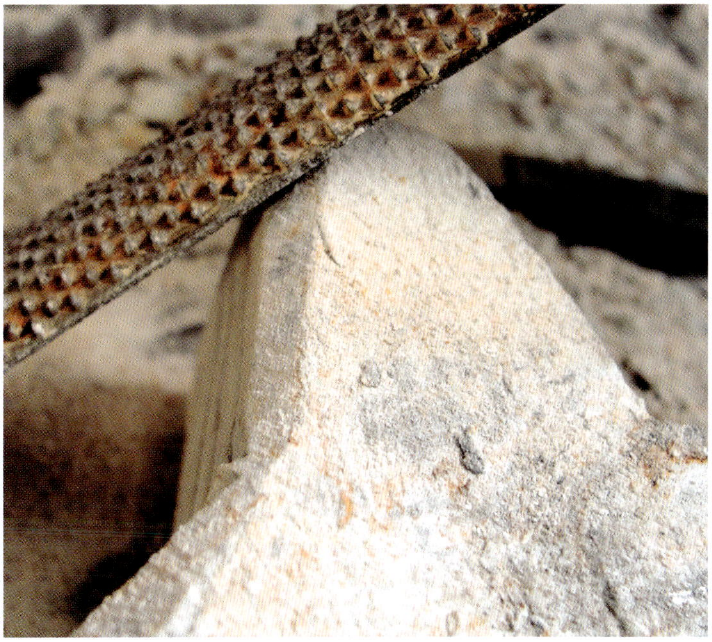

Beginning at the shoulder area start taking off the edges. Follow the line up the jaw to the nose.

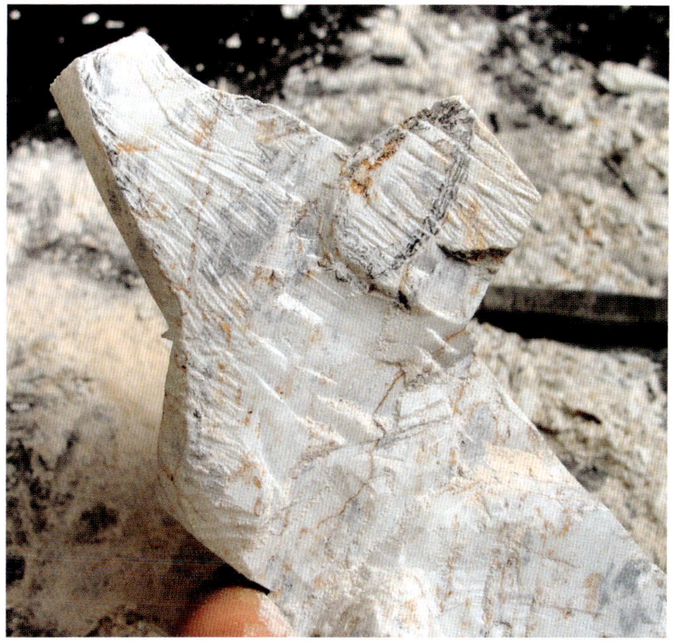

Begin gently rounding the front side of the ear. Continue gently rounding the top of the muzzle. After filing the muzzle, you should have a face profile with a slight indentation creating the forehead.

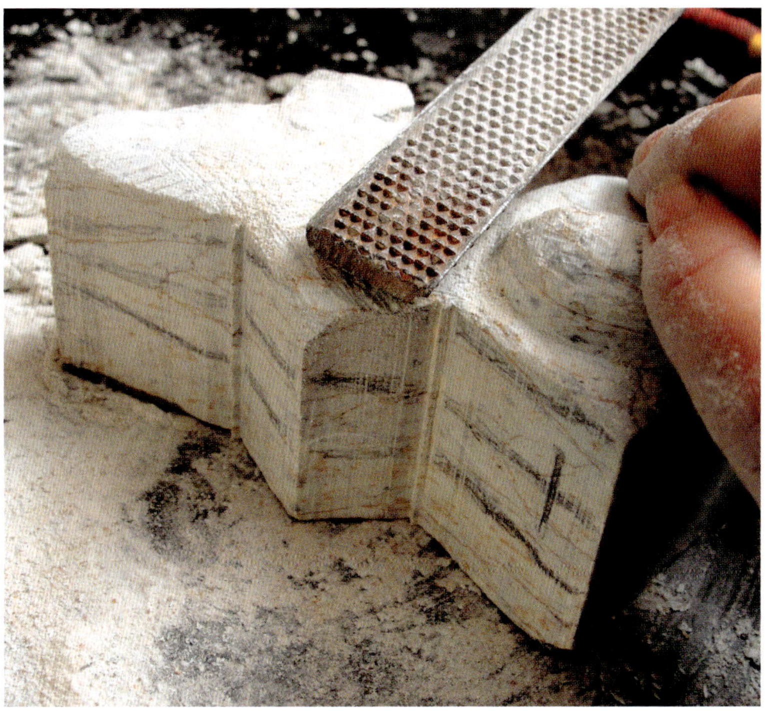

Now file around the back of the ear, taking off the hard edge. Don't remove too much material at this time. At this time you are generally rounding and filing the piece. Here we have moved to the front chest area.

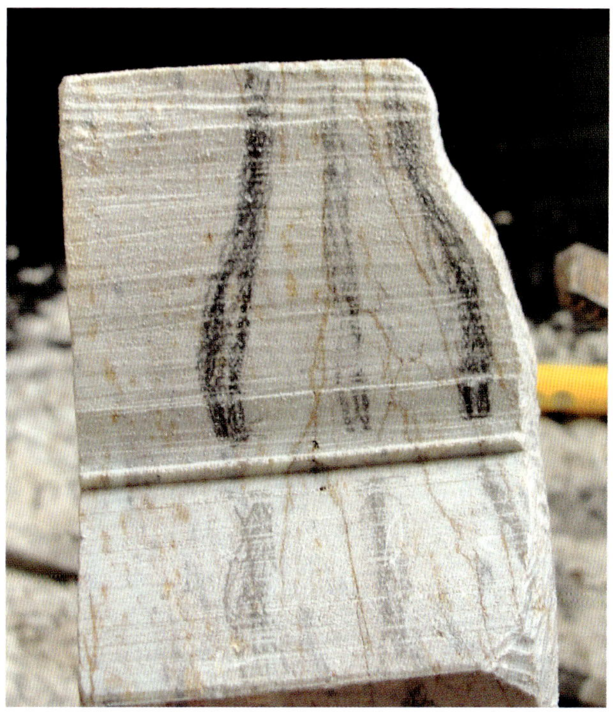

Take a look at the centerline down the front of the chest, and redraw the lines darker if needed. Take the file with the rounded side down to follow the curve of the profile line. Begin removing the excess stone above the line, remembering not to apply too much pressure as the stone will remove quickly and you want to leave some material around the line. It is always possible to remove but difficult to correct if too much stone is removed. At this stage, your piece should look something like this.

Detailing the Design

Here you will redraw the detail of the design. Now that material has been removed, the shape of the coyote starts to emerge and the lines have to be redrawn. With the new lines, you will be able to define what will be the shape of your final coyote.

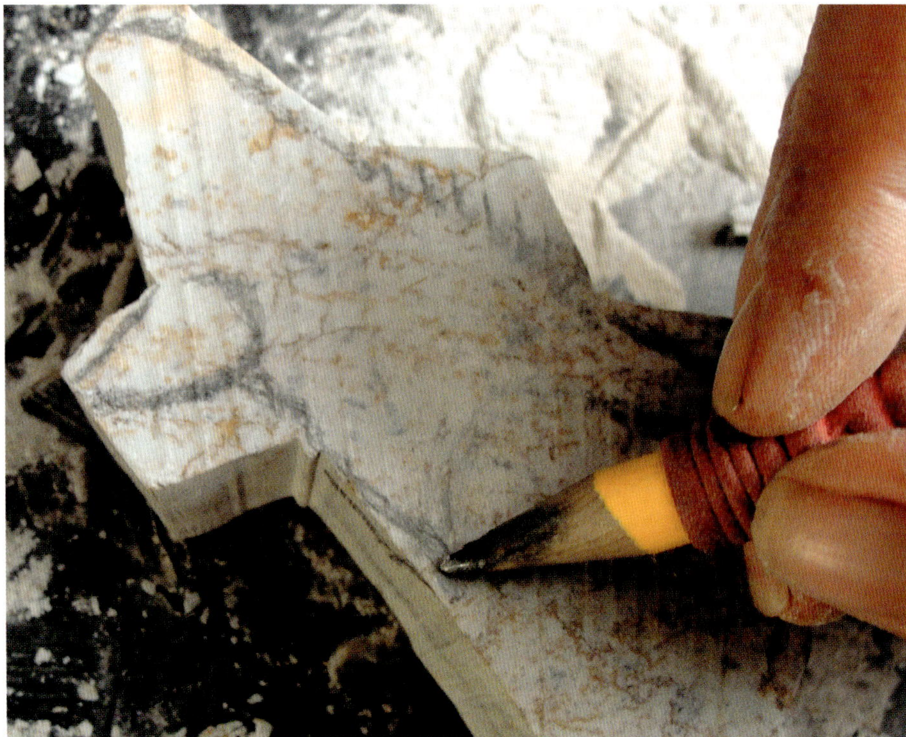

Let's move on to the back with the tail to the left. First, take your pencil and draw in the right shoulder. Once the shoulder has been redefined on the back, turn your piece and draw a straight line, indicating the top of the leg. Using the top line as a guide, begin drawing the curve of the leg. Continue the curve down to form the front of the hind leg; however, do not draw all the way down to the bottom of your piece. Later on you will be forming the hind paw from this area. Draw in the top line for the thickness of the paws. Follow that line around to the side of the piece for the height of the front paw. Now bring the line up to the chest. Take the line straight up to the muzzle, taking into consideration the chest and the chin. Those two points should have a slight curvature. Now look at the point where the ears meet the forehead. Take your pencil and begin creating the area that will be the ear. The ear should be in the shape of a tear drop. Now begin drawing the line that will form the back. Pay attention to the curvature of the hips. Take the line down and curve it in to form the rest of the leg. Here we identify where the body will actually end. Even though it is not a lot of material to remove, it is still a good idea to mark out the detail of the design. Go back to the front of the leg and mark the desired thickness of the paw. Draw in the curve of the paw. Your piece should look something like this.

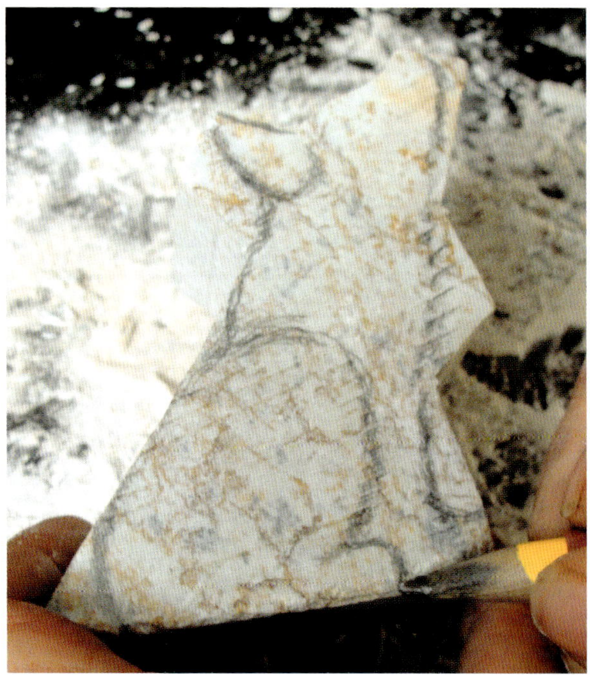

Creating the Leg, Defining the Paw

Here we deal with the leg and techniques of removing stone on the right side of the piece. With the flat chisel you will create the leg and define the ear, jaw, and paw.

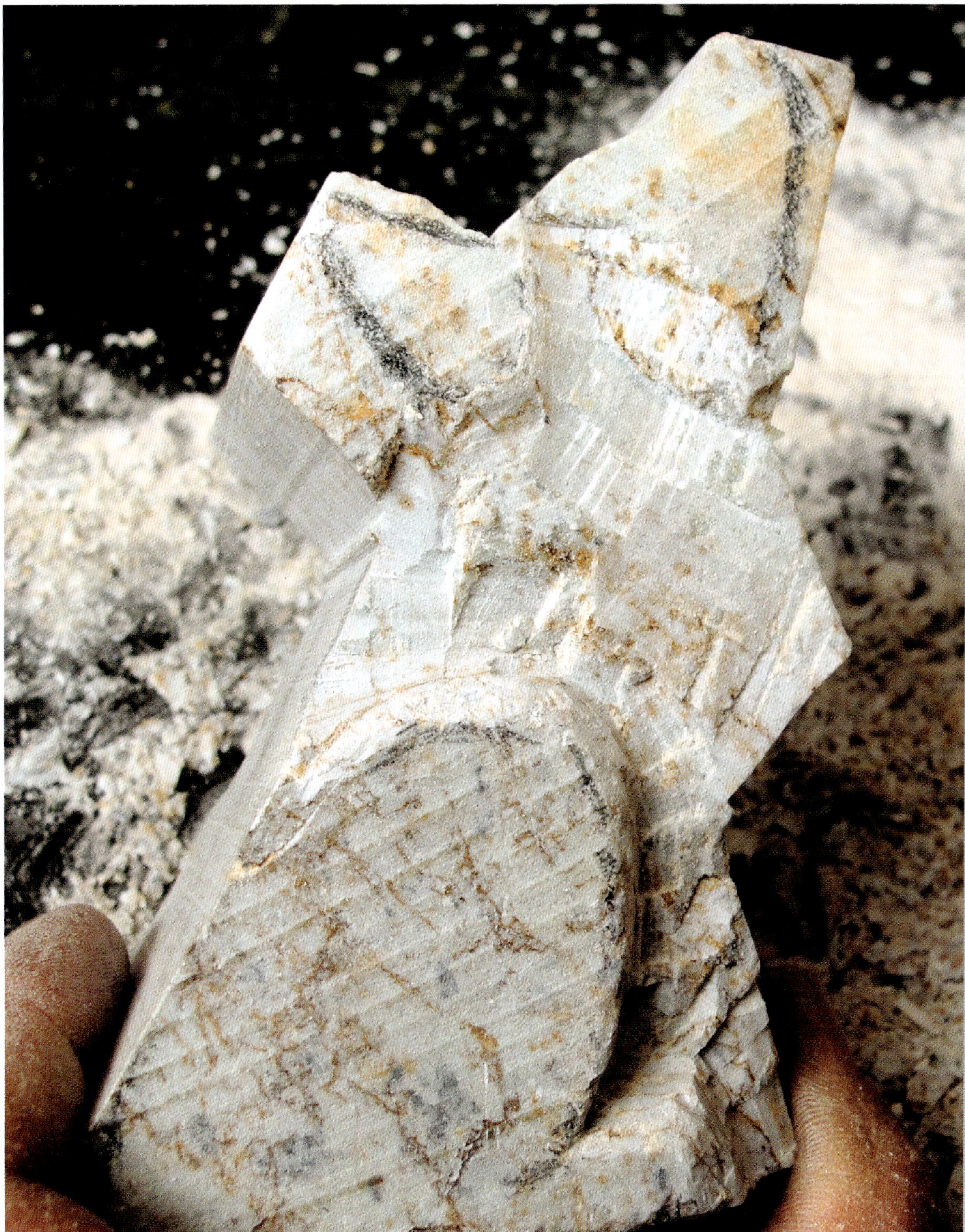

Creating the leg and defining the ear, jaw, and paw.

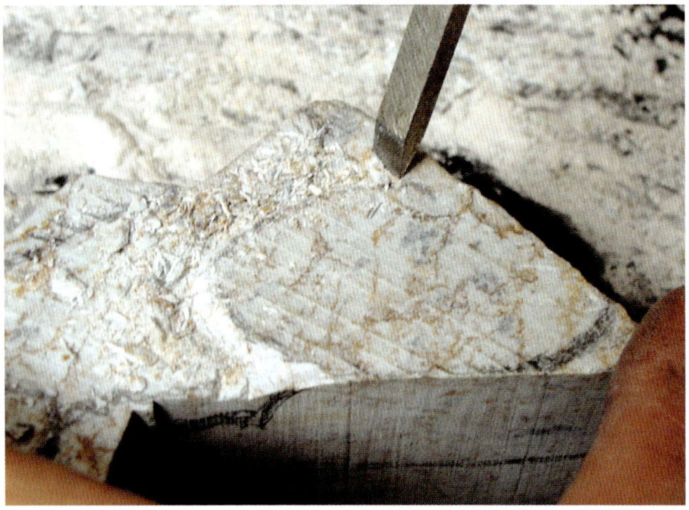

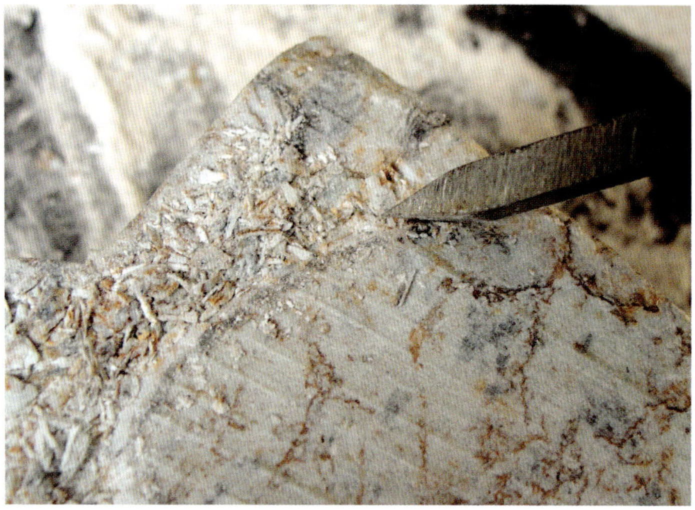

Begin at the top of the leg, where the line meets the back. Stab the corner of the chisel into the stone and twist the chisel in an upward motion. Remove the stone gently. Don't apply too much pressure or stab too deeply. Just follow the line of the leg down to the paw. You will be removing the material in layers as opposed to chunks. Once you have defined the line of the leg on the first pass, continue the same technique for a second pass. Remove another thin layer of material. Continue removing the material in layers until the desired depth is reached.

Stab the chisel in the crease of the paw. Gently twist.

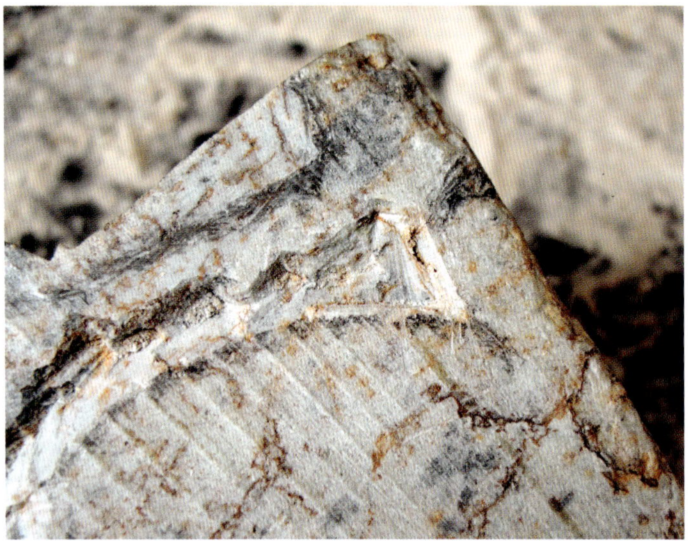

Your leg should now be defined all the way to the top of the paw.

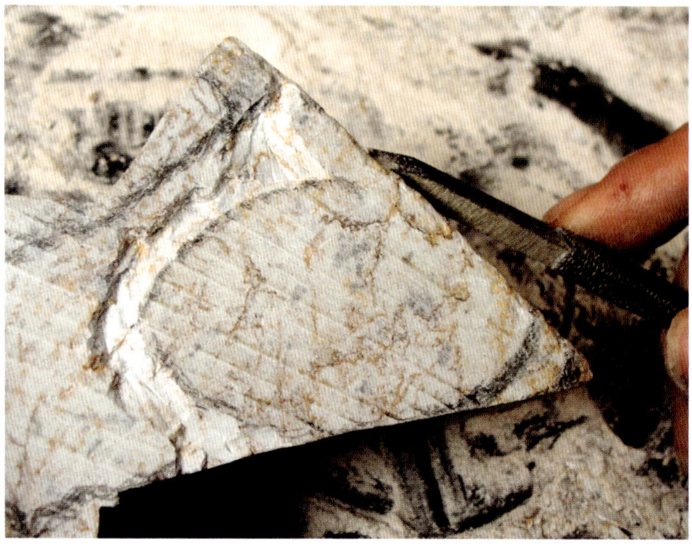

Continue around, creating the paw. Remember not to go too deep at this point.

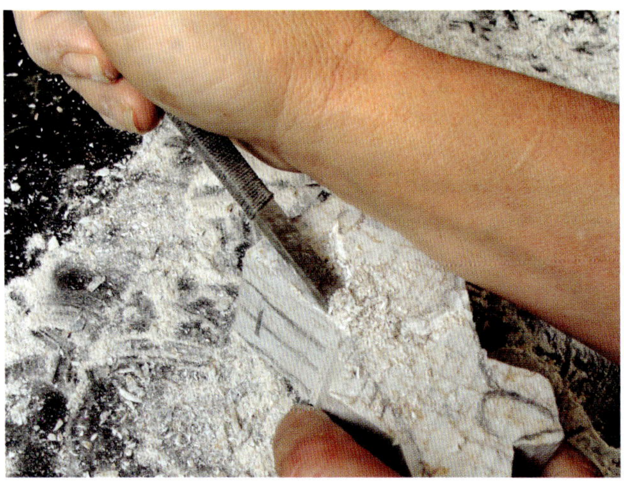

Now that the leg and paw are defined, take the chisel and begin removing the material deeper and further out from the leg. Here the chisel is held at an angle, facing the body, at roughly a twenty-degree angle from the stone. This technique is accomplished by almost not moving the wrist but moving the arm towards the body. The chisel's angle planes the stone and removes material in a light, even manner. By subtracting the stone, you are creating the dimension of the leg and paw. You may want to do a few strokes first until you are comfortable with the technique.

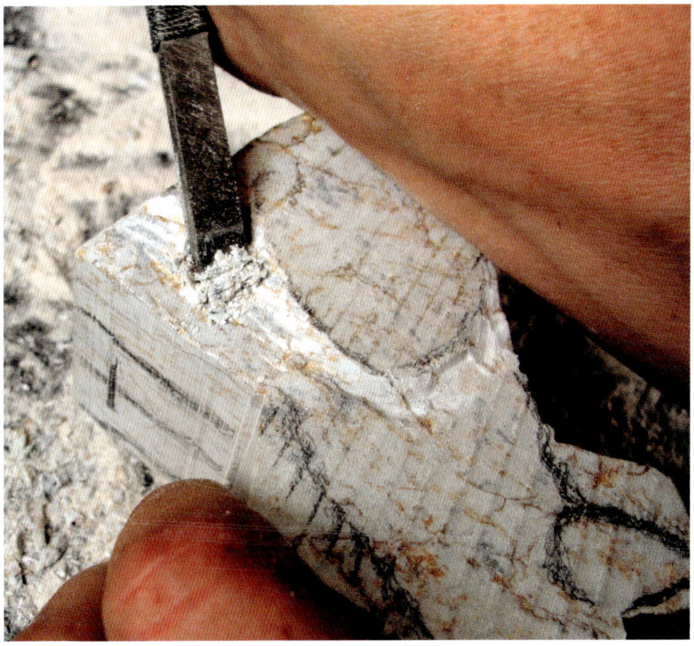

If you tilt the chisel's angle higher, the cut will be deeper.

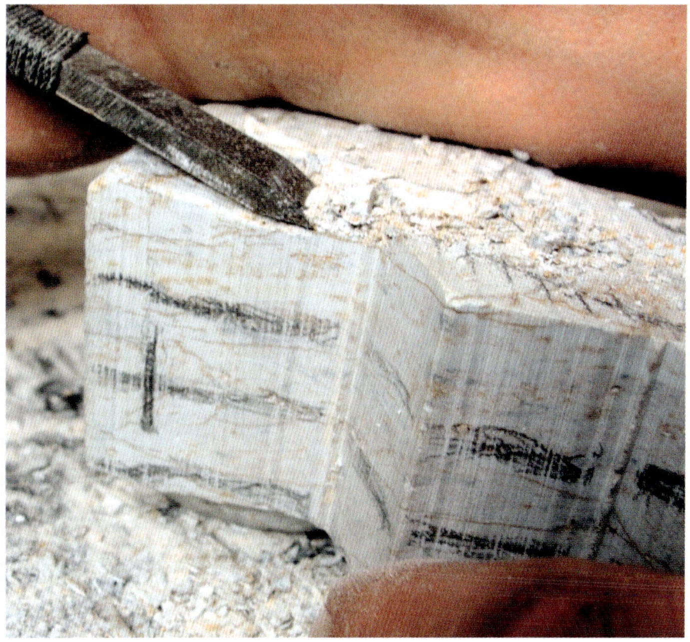

We call this the snow plow because, as you can see here, the material piles up on the chisel like snow.

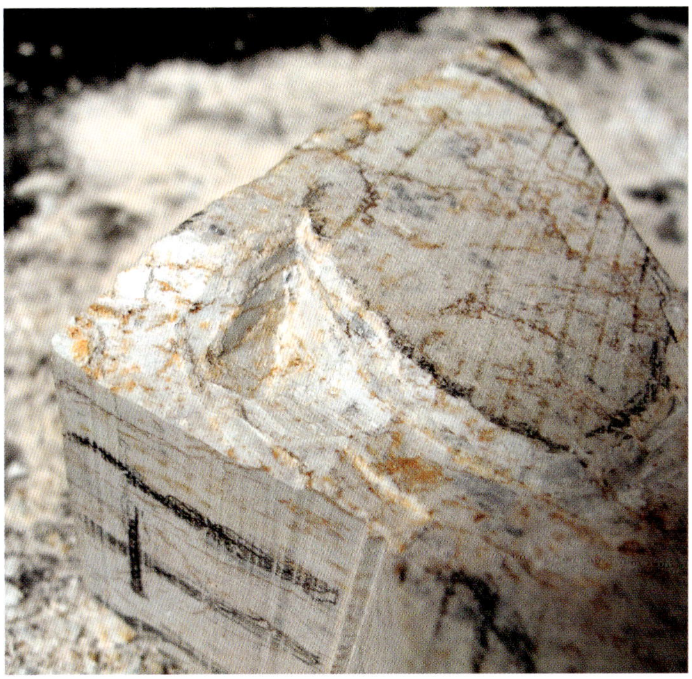

Return to the crease of the paw to further define it. Take a step back and look at your piece. It should look something like this.

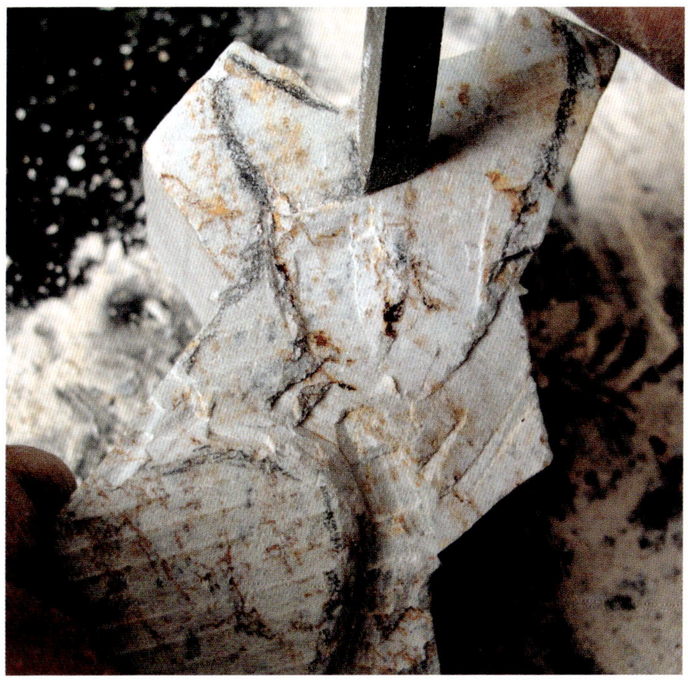

Using the same technique remove material in the chest area. Before moving on to the ears, take another look at the paw and remove any material necessary. In this case, we defined the tip of the paw a little bit more. Gently plane away material by the ears. Don't go too deep.

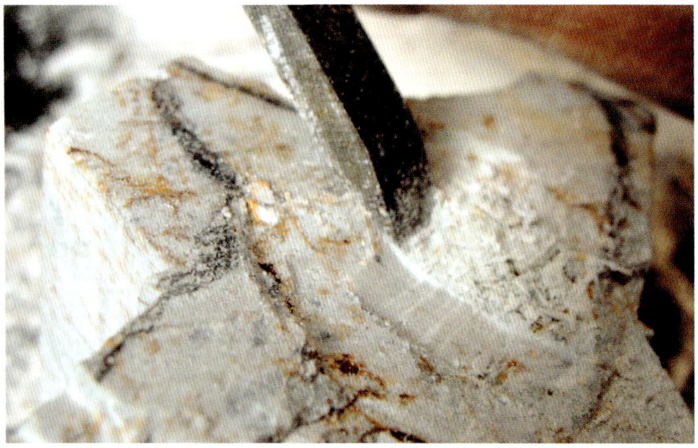

Now define the jaw line, lightly.

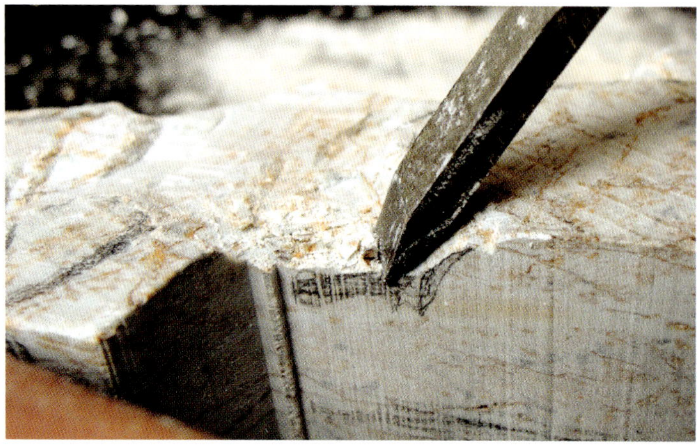

On the side view, below the ear, dig out material with the tip of the chisel until you get to the line. Be sure not to dig too deep past the line. Switch sides and work from the other angle on the shoulder. Again, apply gentle pressure on the chisel and remove the material in an upward motion.

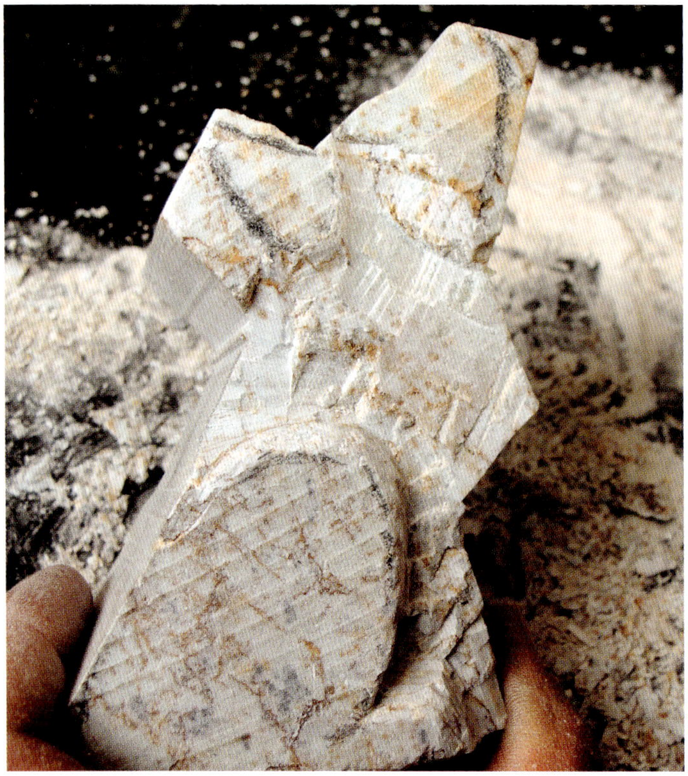

Take a step back and look at the piece. You should have a well defined leg and paw. The ear and the jaw are being defined as well but not as deep.

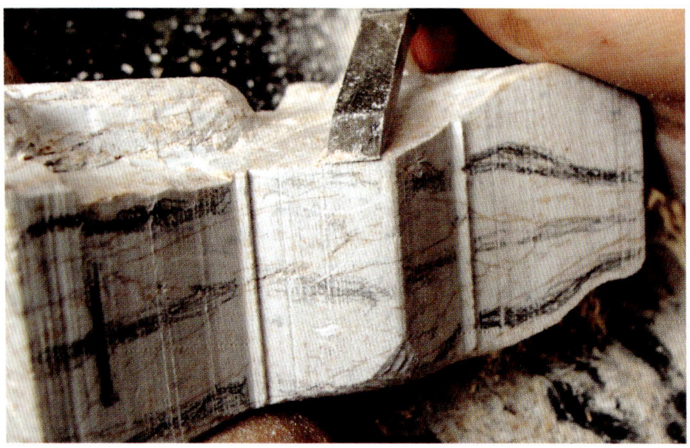

Continue to plane the piece to smooth out the stone, being careful, again, not to go too deep. But do go all the way to the edge.

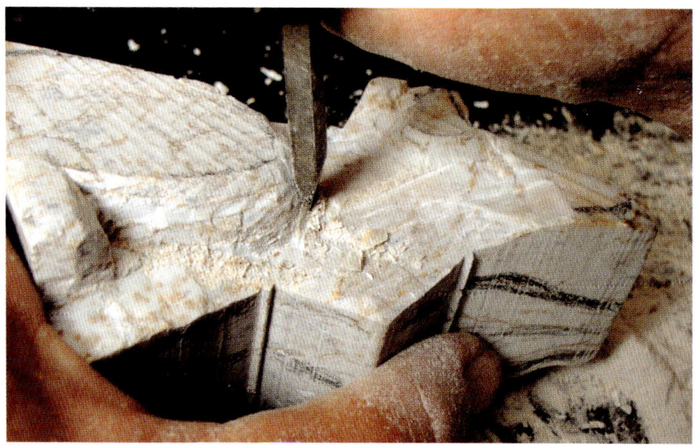

Here we are removing even more material for the definition of the leg and the paw. Work on any areas that define the leg to make sure that it is well defined.

Creating the Head

Here we focus on defining the head.

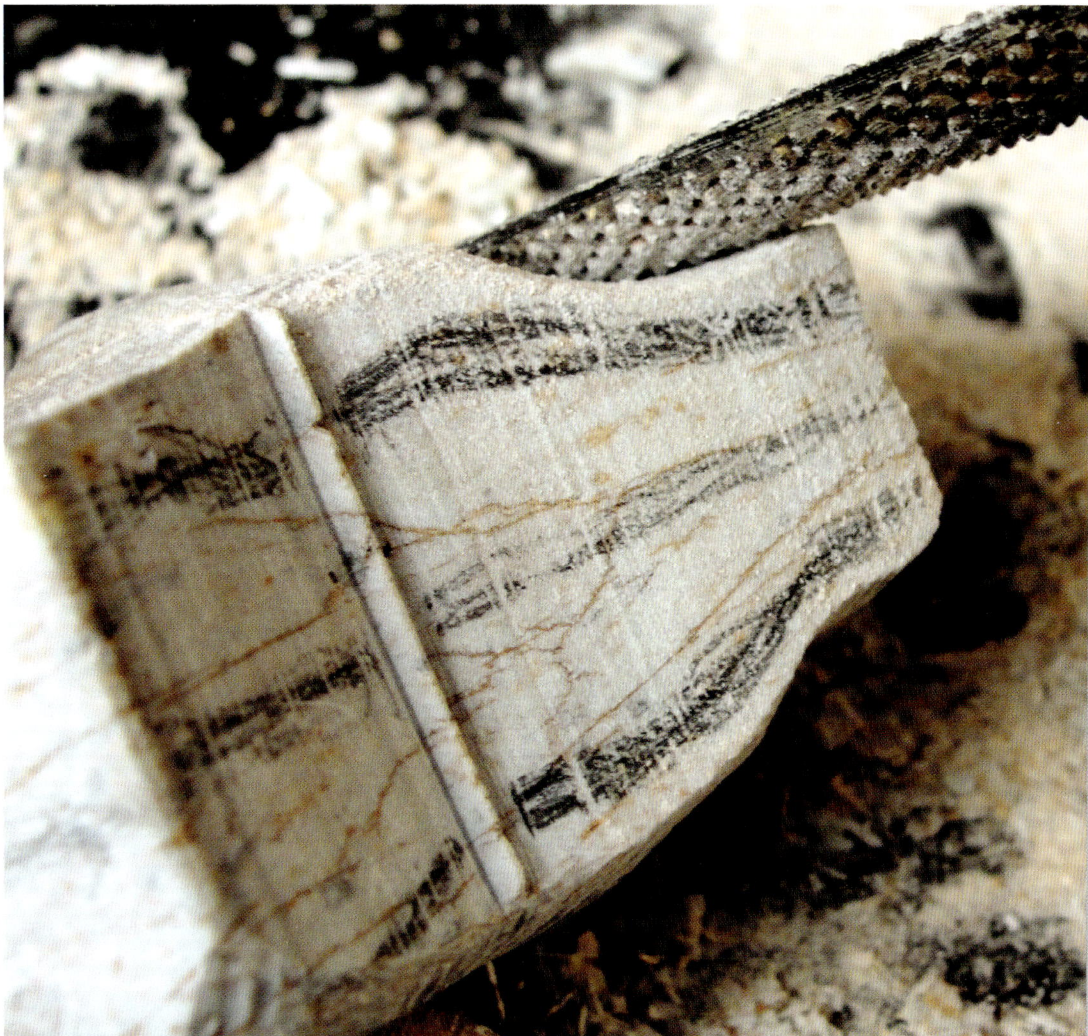

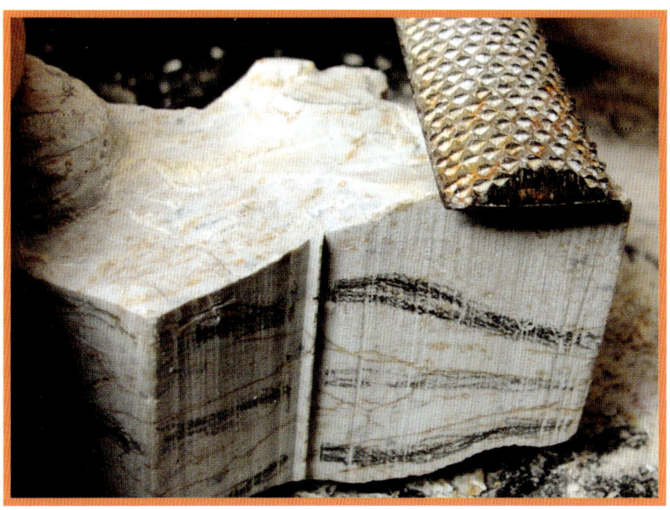

Take the four-sided file. Tilt the piece on its side and begin with the flat side of the file on the piece. Remove material in a sweeping motion.

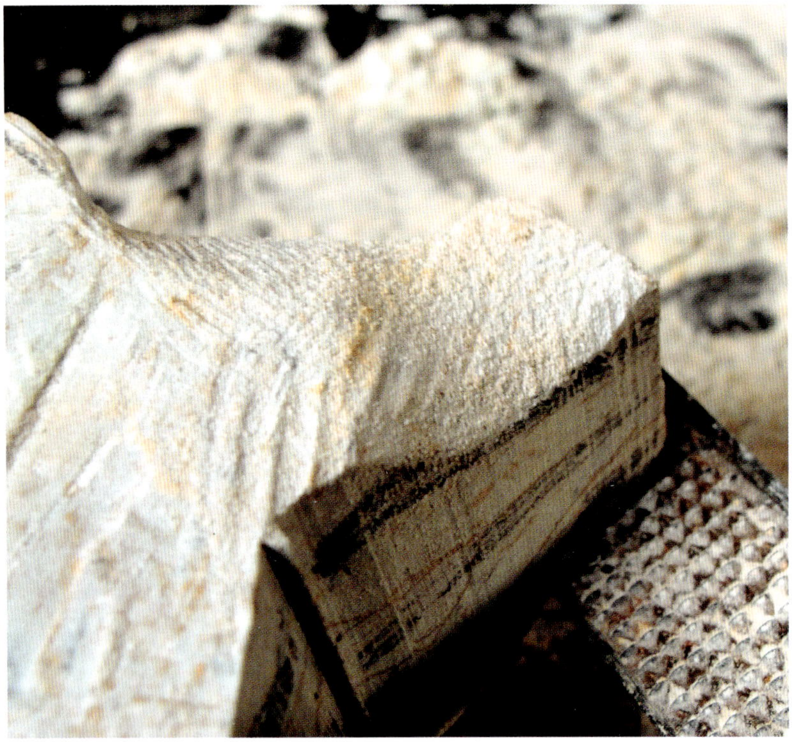

As you approach the line, flip the file over to the rounded side to create the curve of the muzzle. By creating the muzzle, you will see definition that will eventually create the jaw.

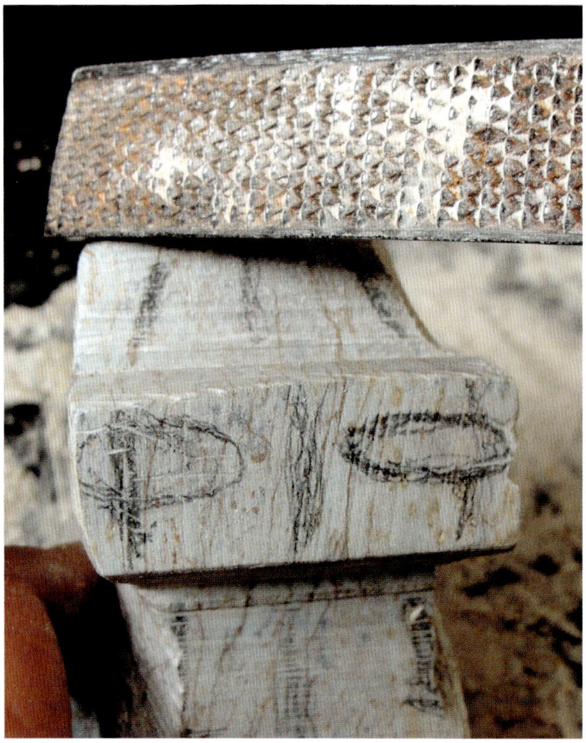

Stand the piece up and gently round the edges of the muzzle.

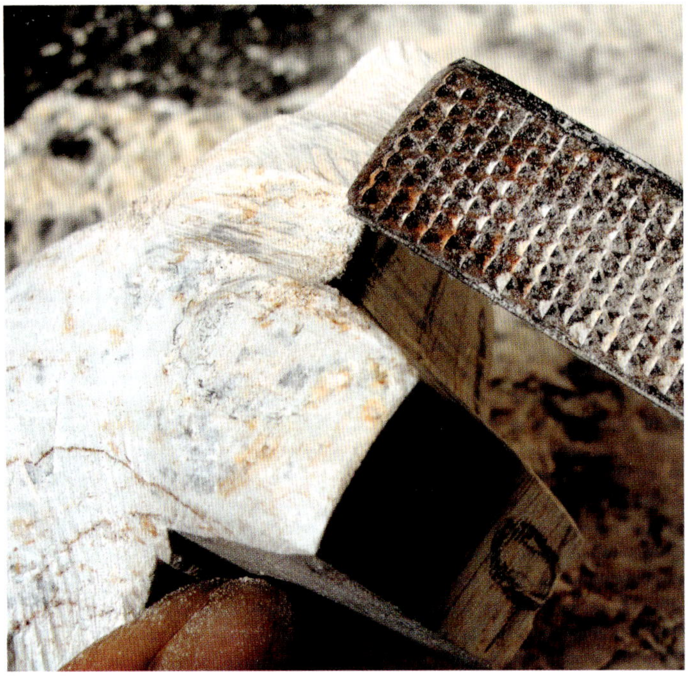

With the piece on its side again, and using the edge of the four-sided file, make one deep swipe at the ear. It should look like this, adding definition to the head.

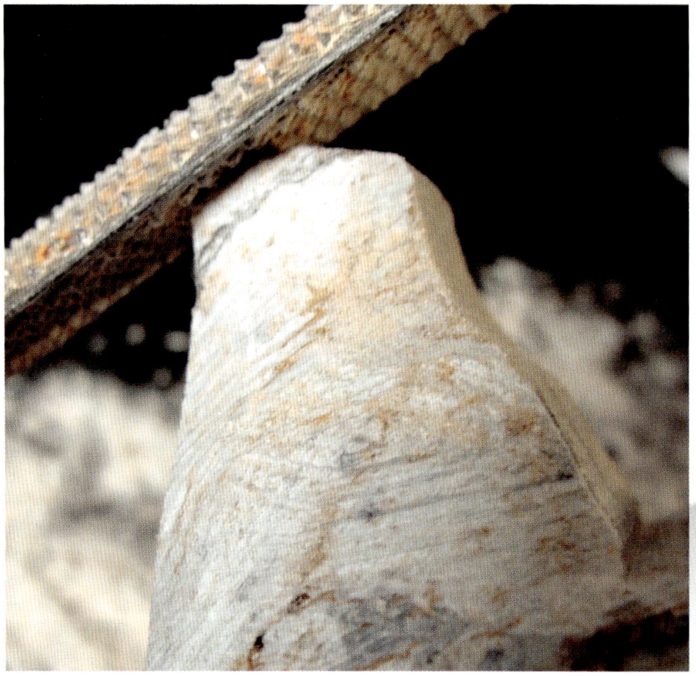

Looking at the muzzle from the side, take your pencil and draw a line to identify the angle you choose for the muzzle. As we mentioned before, you might want to look ahead at the photographs to see how we formed the tip of the muzzle. In this photograph, you can see the side angle as well as the flat part of the muzzle. Define that angle and you end up with the nose and mouth. Be careful not to go too far; stay just above the line.

Rounding the Body

This section encompasses all the rounding and some of the finishing details of the coyote. This is where the piece really comes alive. Again, we encourage you to look ahead at the photographs before you start any stage.

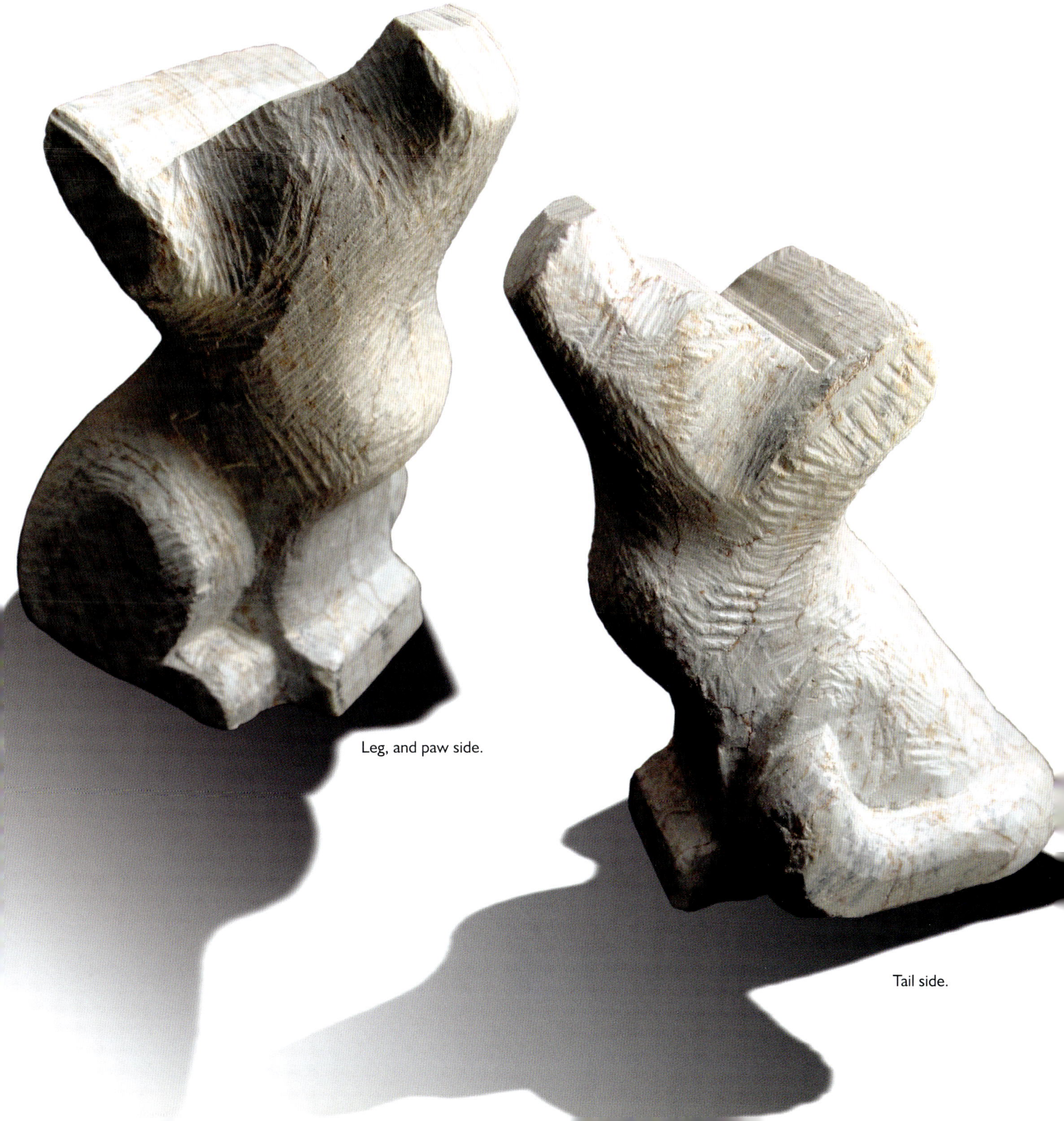

Leg, and paw side.

Tail side.

Take a moment to look at the piece

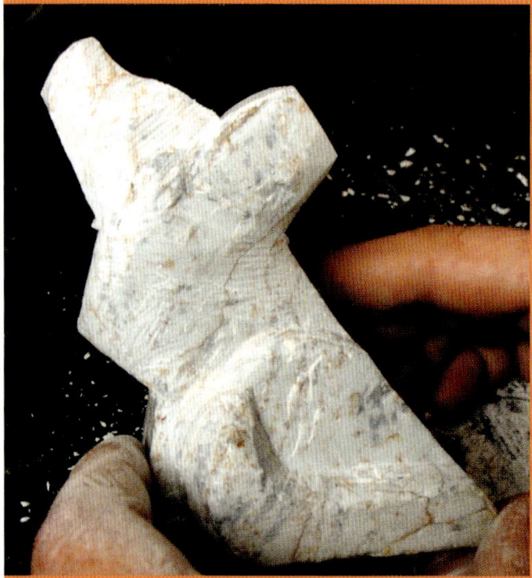

Here is the tail side.

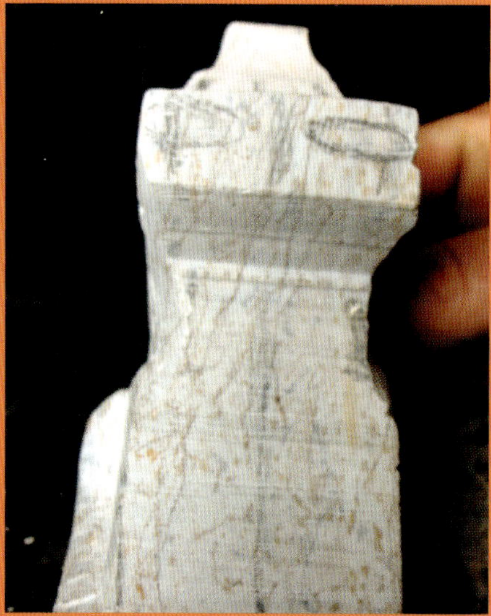

View from the top.

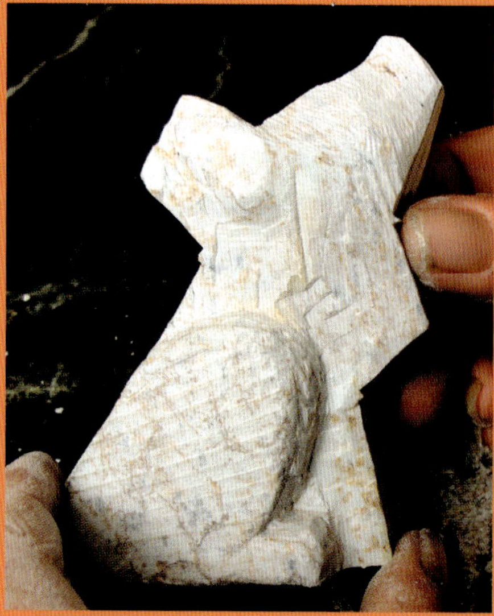

Leg and paw side.

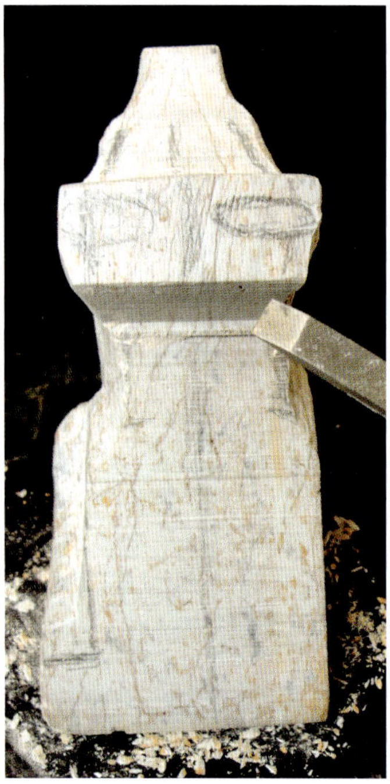

To make sure your contours are even on both sides, stay conscious of the centerline down the back at all times. Next you will be working on the neck line.

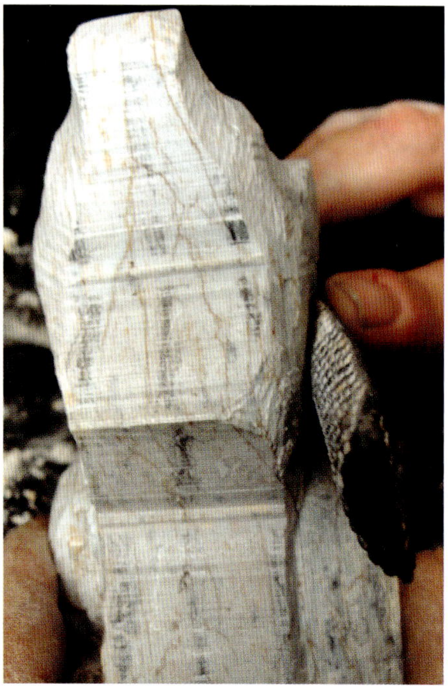

Turning the piece around, start the base of the jaw using your four-sided file and round the side down. Begin filing by gently removing material.

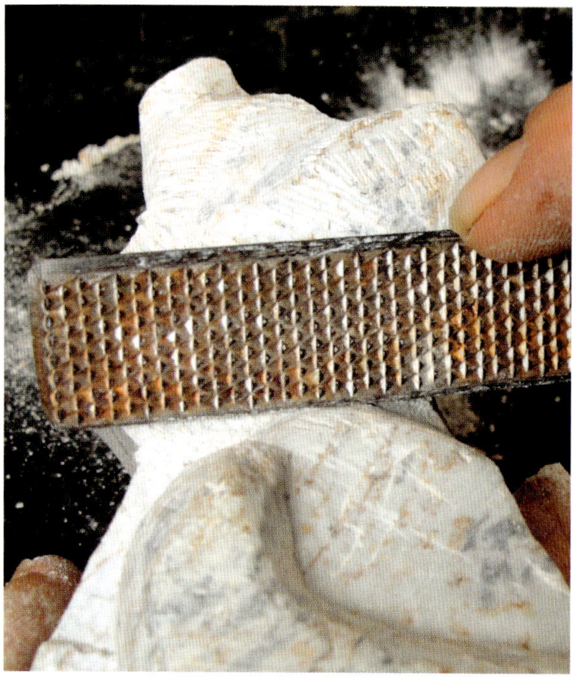

Be careful under the ear. Gently file above the ear as well. You are gently rounding the shoulder area in a rocking motion, from side to side.

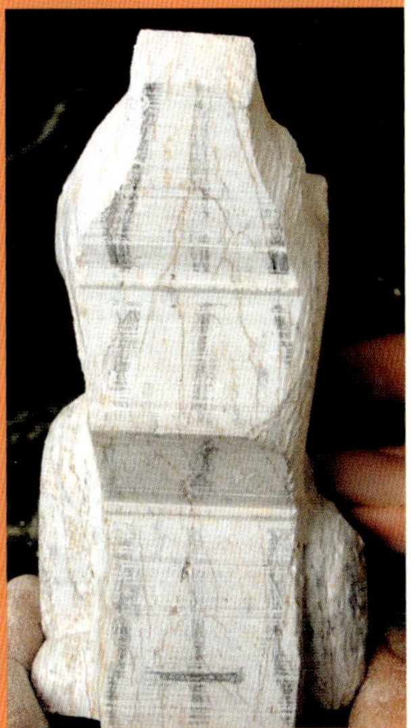

Chest view.

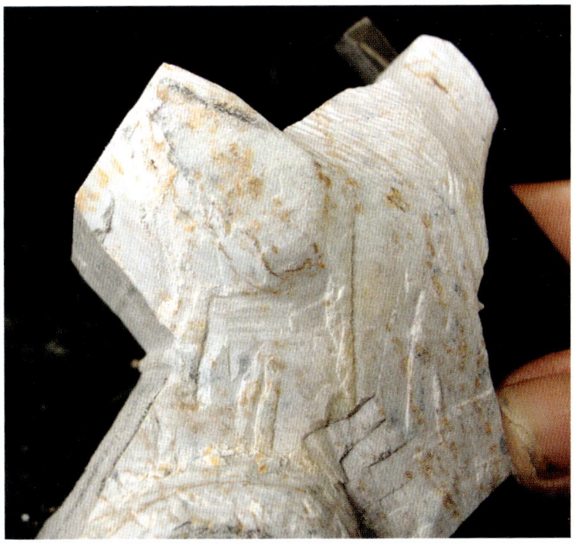

Begin behind the ear: with the chisel remove material gently and slowly around the ear. Clean off the piece frequently so that you can see where you are. Make sure you do not remove too much material.

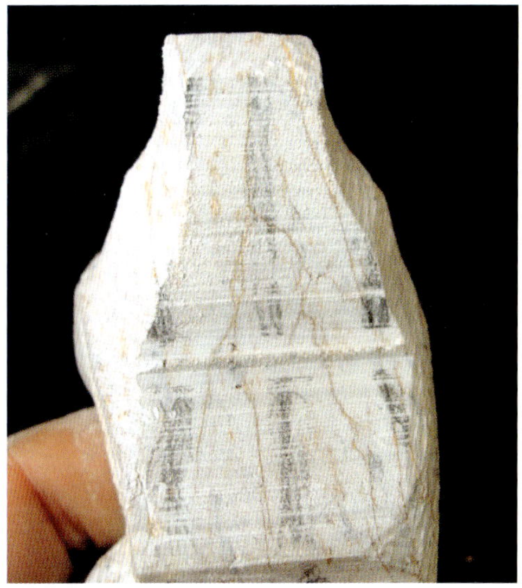

Once the ear is defined, move on to the chest view of the coyote and grab your file. Starting at the base of the jaw line, begin removing material in a upward sweeping motion, along the line. The jaw appears to flatten out, but it is softening the edge of the neckline. Repeat on both sides. Now compare your piece to this photo.

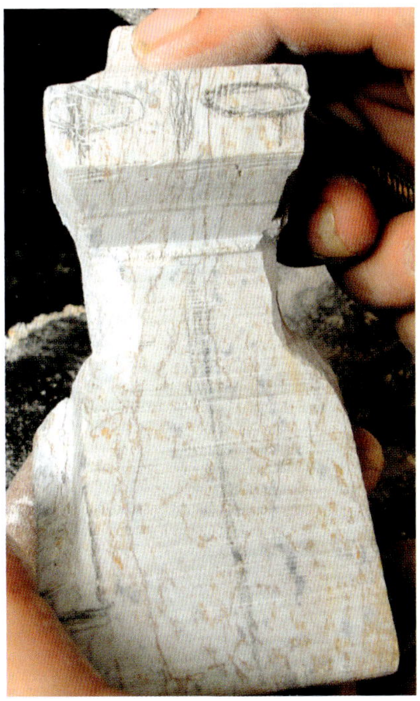

Here you can see the definition of the neckline beginning to appear.

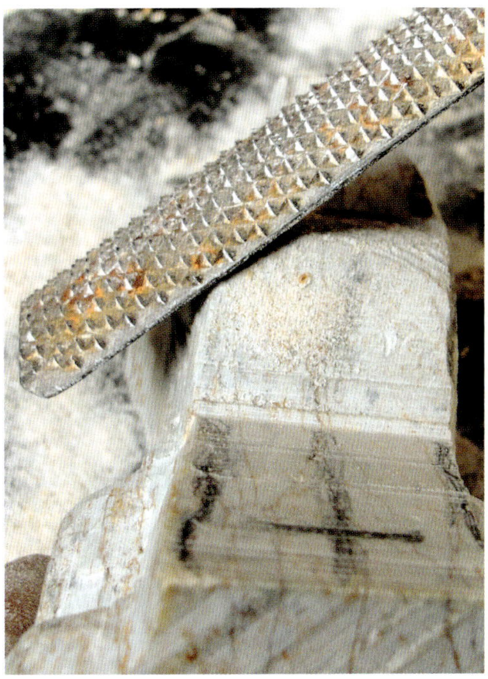

Tilt your piece to the side, tail side up, and redraw the chest line if needed. Take the file, flat side down, and gently file the angle off the chest. Repeat on the other side, rocking the file over to the left.

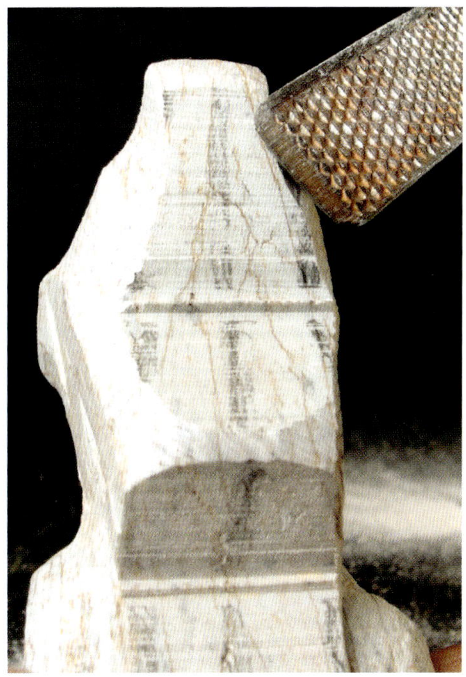

Stand the piece up. Your piece should look something like this.

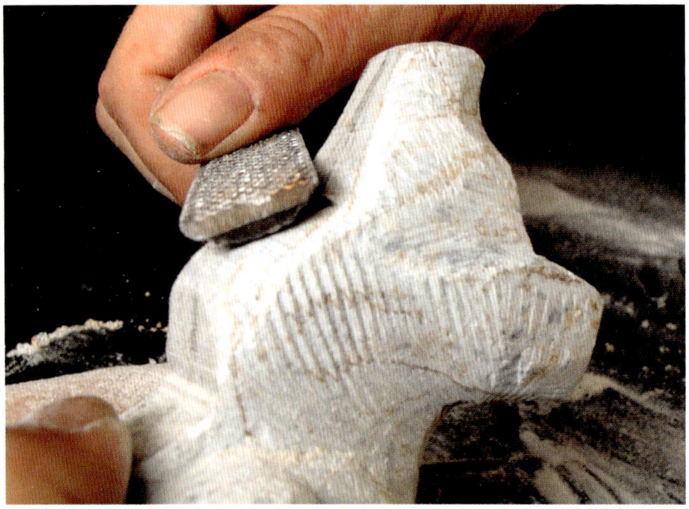

With the file round side down, round under the jaw in a sweeping motion. You can alternate to the flat side of the file to create the contour of the chest. Here below the jaw line you can see the chest begin to appear.

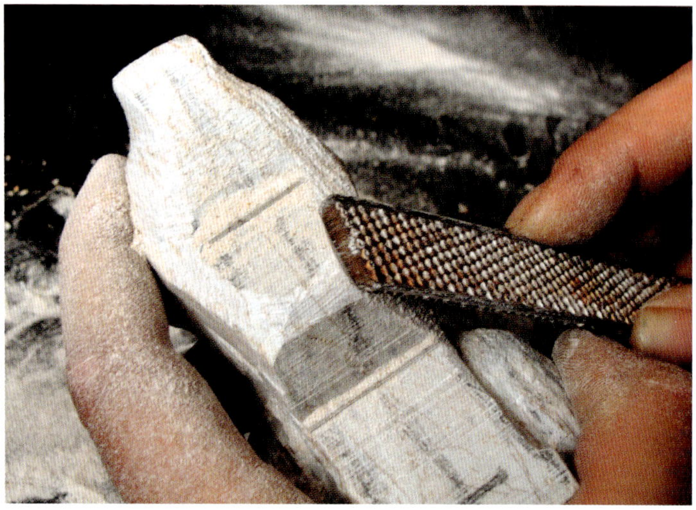

Continue rounding the neck and jaw line. Start at the base of the jaw in the chest area. Move upward and then back down. Repeat on the other side.

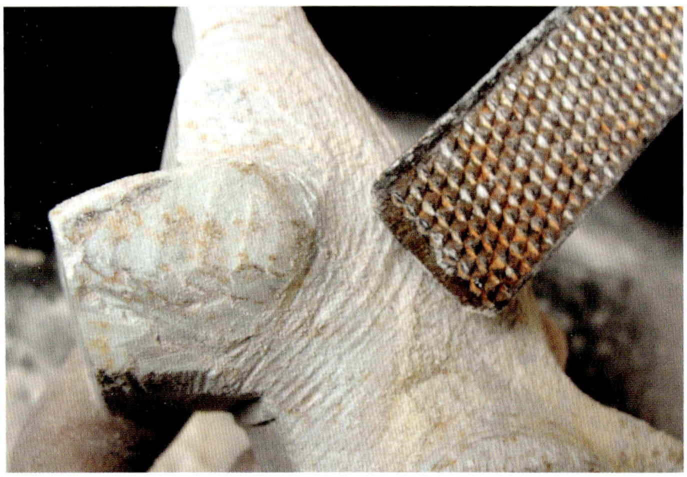

Now pay close attention to the ear. Using the round side of the file, starting at the top of the head, make a downward sweep around the outline of the ear. Here you can see the file lines clearly defining the ear as well as the neck. Continue rounding the ear and neck area.

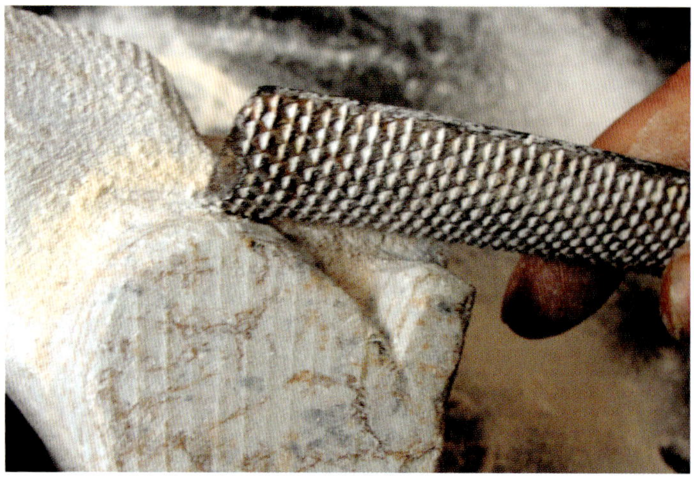

To work the piece evenly, take a break from the neck and move down to the leg.

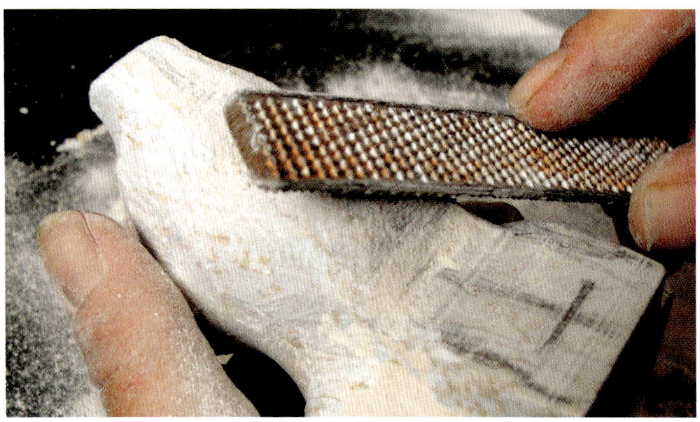

Now move over to the chest and work on smoothing the hard edges there. Little by little, the shape of the coyote emerges.

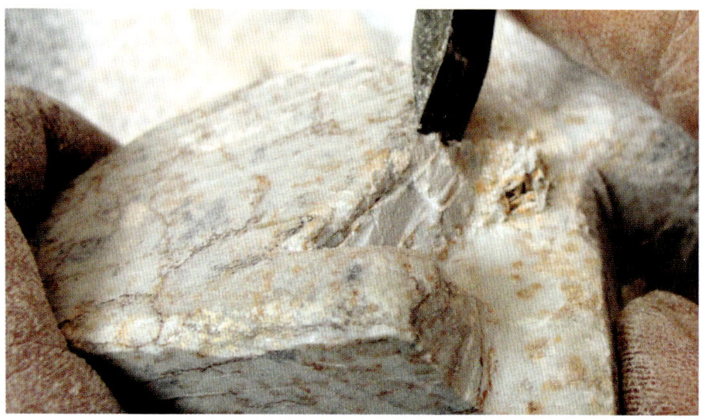

At this point, should you desire, you can define the leg and paw area even deeper. Using your flat chisel in a rocking motion, chip away more stone at an angle for more definition.

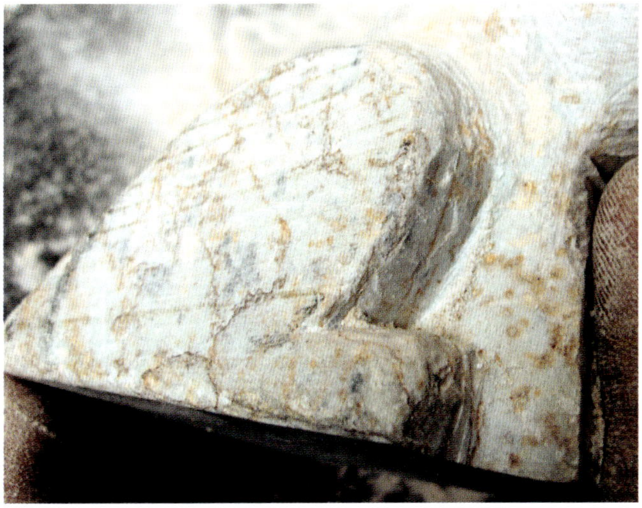

Work it slow. See how much more prominent the leg and paw become.

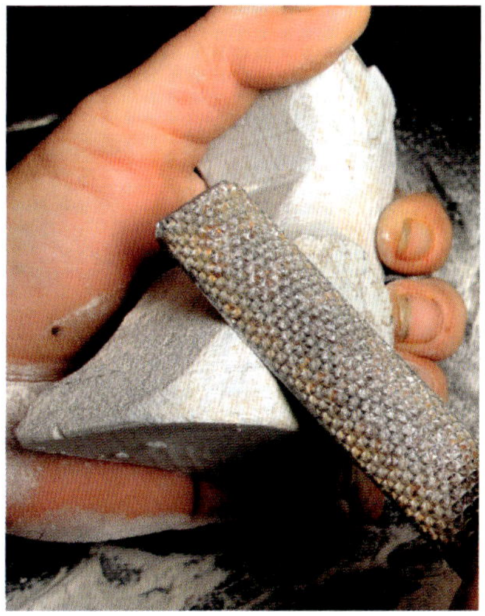

Go back to the file and begin filing off the edge on the back side. Using the flat side of the file, once again, follow the line removing material at an angle. See how the edge flattens out. Once the initial edge is flattened, it takes just a little motion to round it out.

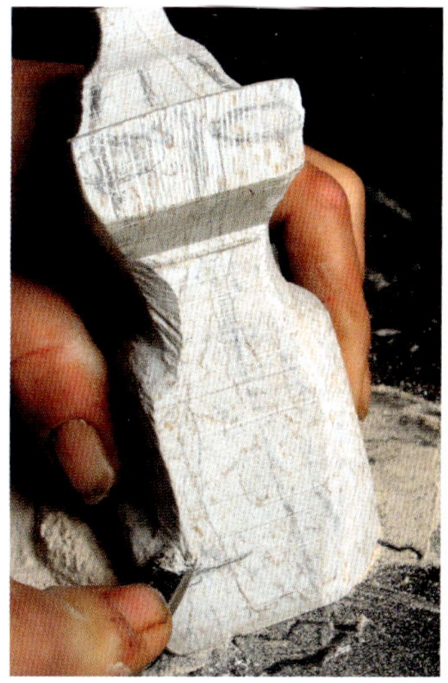

Note the difference between the two sides. Before beginning to round out the tail side of the coyote define where the tail meets the body.

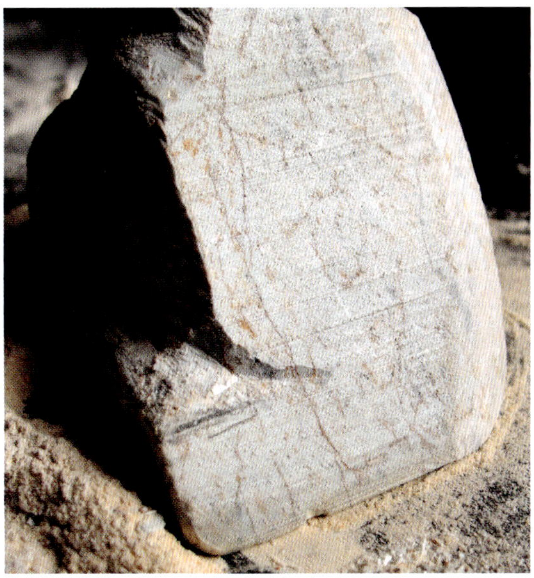

Gently chip out the line with the chisel. This is what your piece should look like.

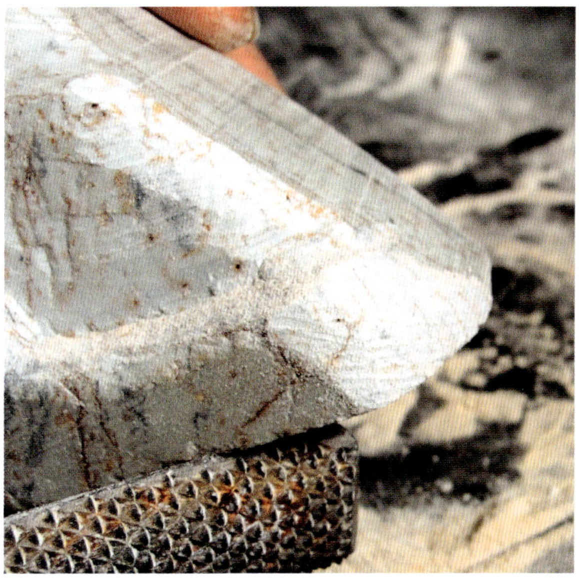

Now with the file take off the hard edge above the line you just created. Follow it up the body. Be sure to round out the corners. Contour the base of the piece.

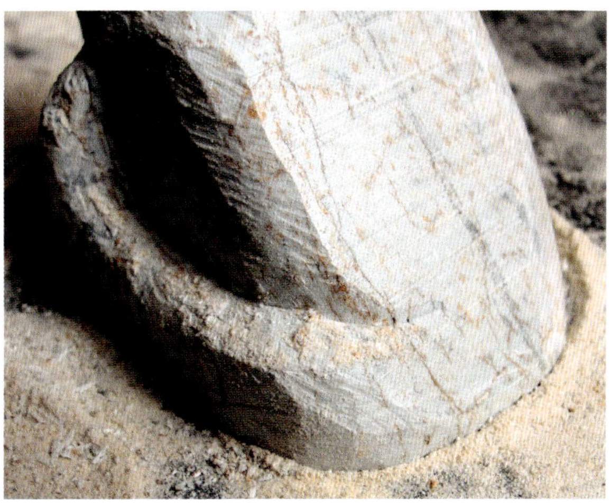

Now that you have rounded the base, you may want to define the tail a bit more. Using the chisel, work the back line. Your piece should look like this.

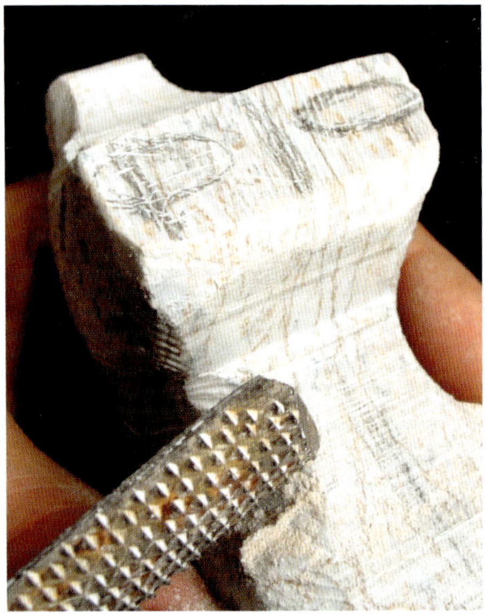

Continue rounding the body. Gently swipe the back of the ears to eliminate the hard edge. It should like this.

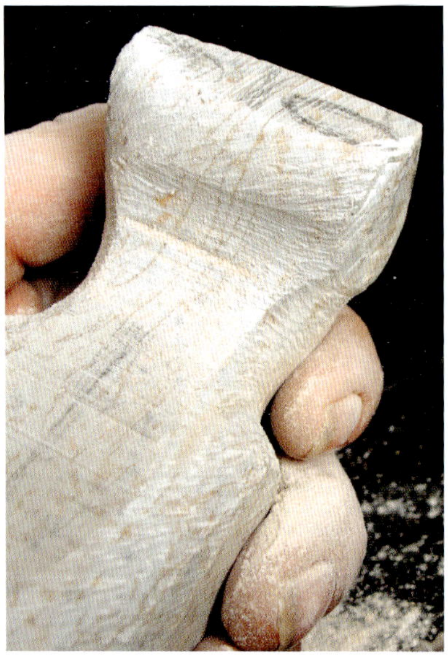

Begin rounding the outer corners of the ears. Emphasize the neck area as you go. The neck becomes more defined as the hard lines fade away.

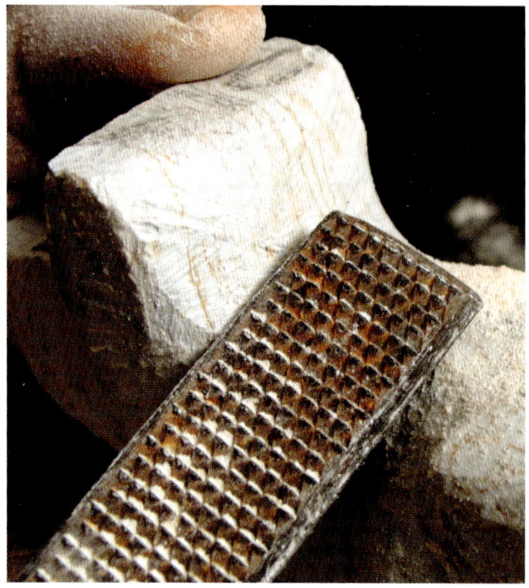

Take your file to remove the material until the centerline disappears.

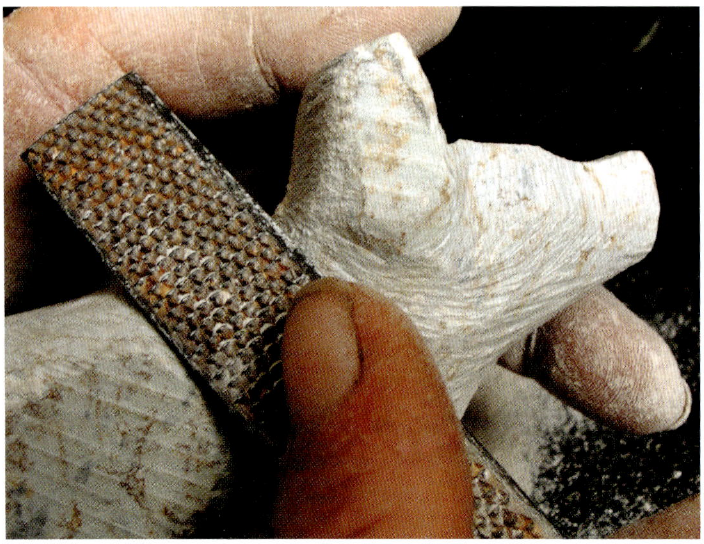

Short back and forth strokes behind the ears and above the shoulder will create the neckline. Go back to working behind the ears on the other side. It is important to grip your piece firmly and apply short "rubbing" motions to the stone.

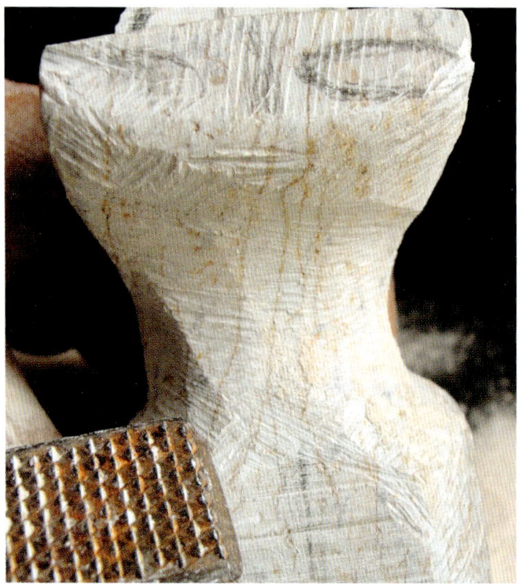

Continue rounding, delicately the back of the coyote. The curve of the file should almost match the curve of the neckline. Be careful not to remove too much. Repeat on the other side.

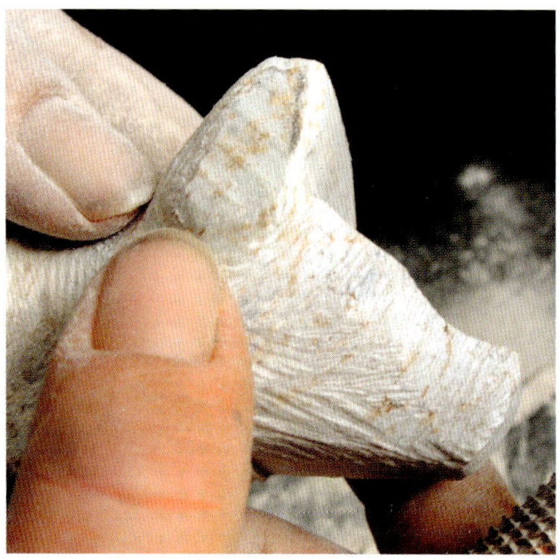

Back to the ears. Here is where you have to be really careful. While supporting the neck, begin to slowly remove the material. The side view of the ear should now look something like this.

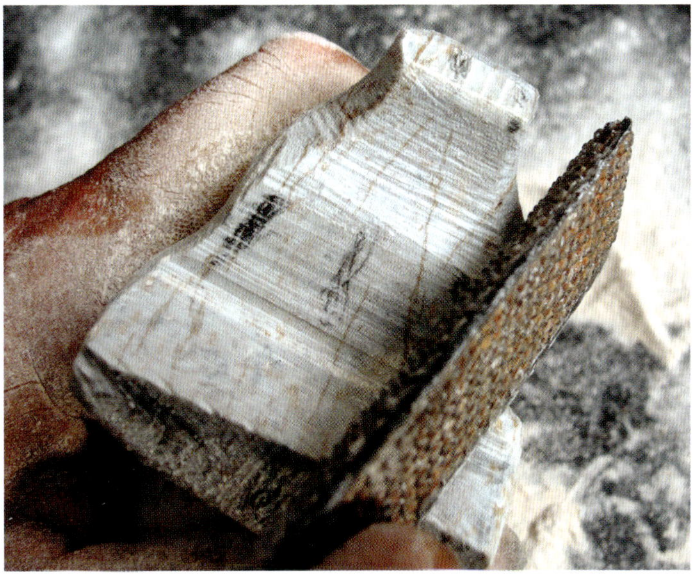

Working from the top view and supporting the head, work gently on the sides of the face.

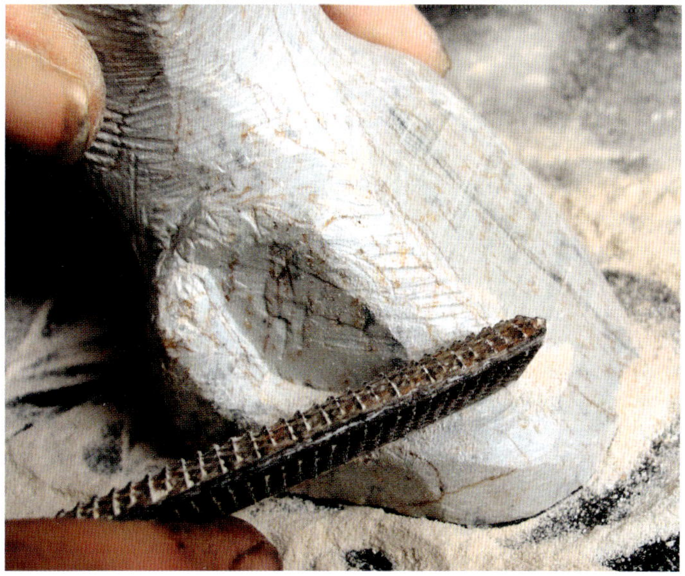

We chose at this point to continue rounding the side of the coyote. Starting at the top of the tail, gently remove the edge and once again round out the back of the coyote.

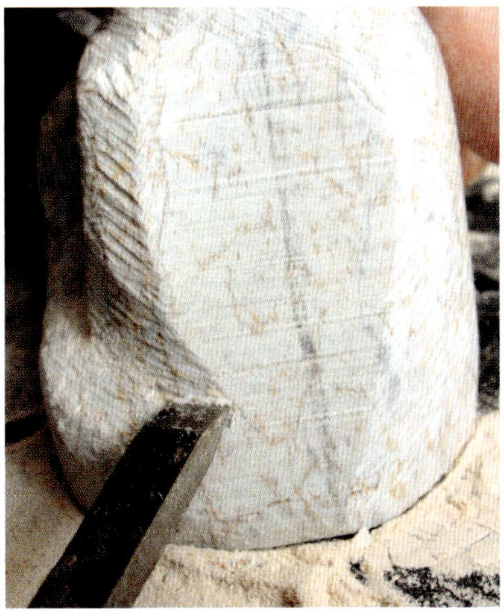

At this point, using your chisel, you can create more definition at the tail. Notice your centerline, one side of the coyote is still broader than the other. By extending the line of the tail, we balance out both sides of the back. Smooth out the tail and the new line with the flat part of the chisel.

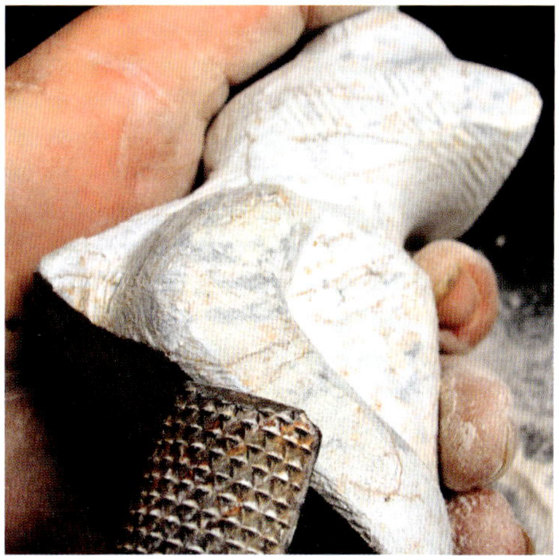

Take your file to round the tail. Continue rounding the tail and the side of the back. You are creating more definition in the tail. Move on to the front of the tail, emphasizing the tail's curve. The rounded edge gives the tail a more natural look.

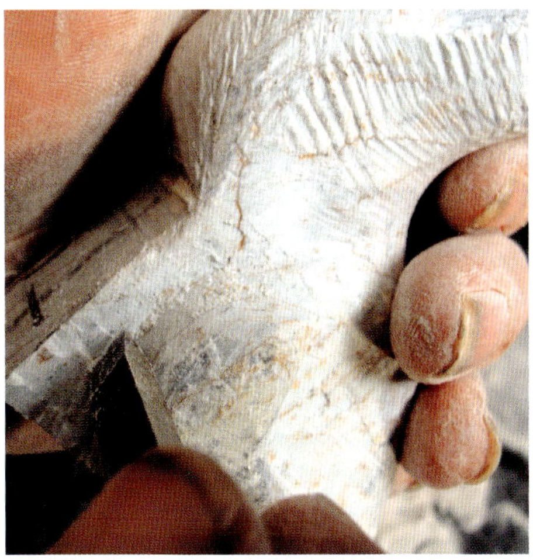

Take the chisel and, with the flat side, remove any additional material by the tip of the tail. You are looking for a smooth and round look around the tail. With the chisel, work up the side of the tail to add more definition. Move up the to the top of the tail. Take the flat side of the chisel and softly round the tail tip.

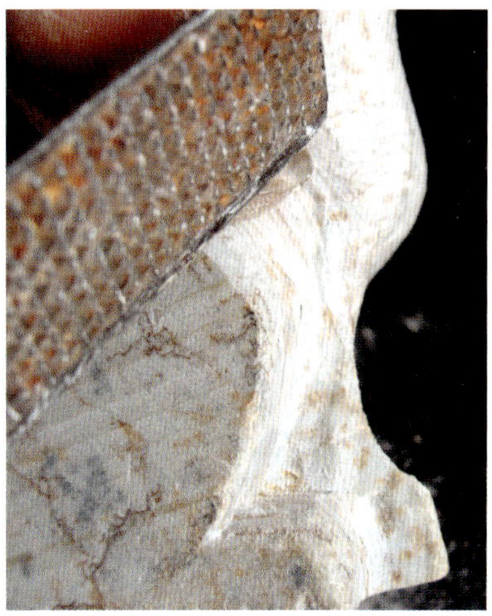

Now turn your piece to the front and note the top line for the front paws. With the chisel, define the top line of the paws. Using your four-sided file, curved side down, begin creating the indentation for the curvature of the coyote's legs. Continue removing material until the desired depth is reached. Here is the profile view of the new curve.

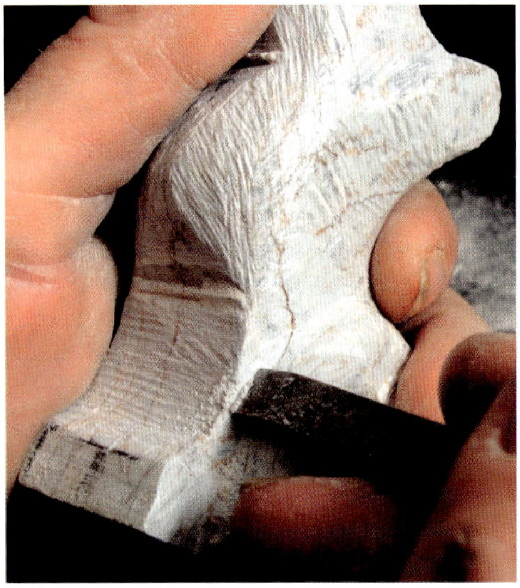

Using your chisel, begin softening the lines of the paws. Work your way up the legs, careful not to remove too much material.

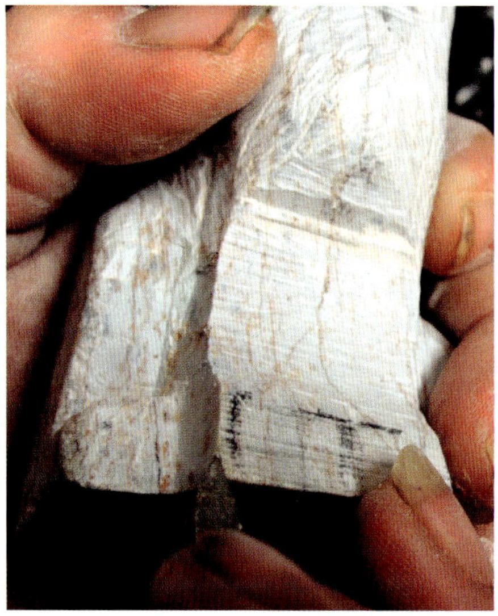

Repeat on the other side. Remove more material around the left paw to better define the lines. Here is the front view of the paws.

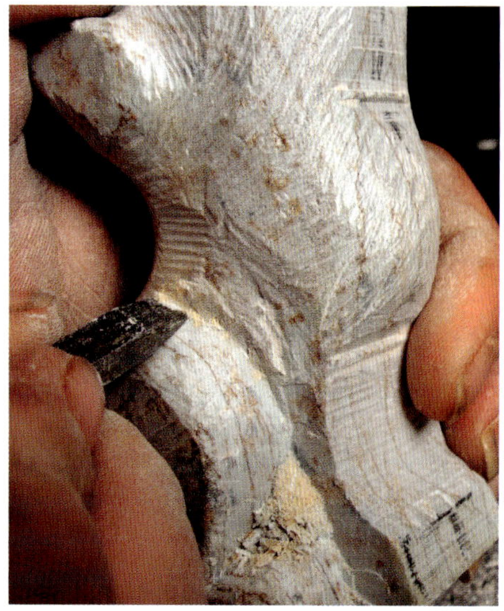

You can use the chisel to scrape along the back leg. Define the line all the way to the top. Continue working on the details of the lines above the leg using small movements so as not to gouge the stone.

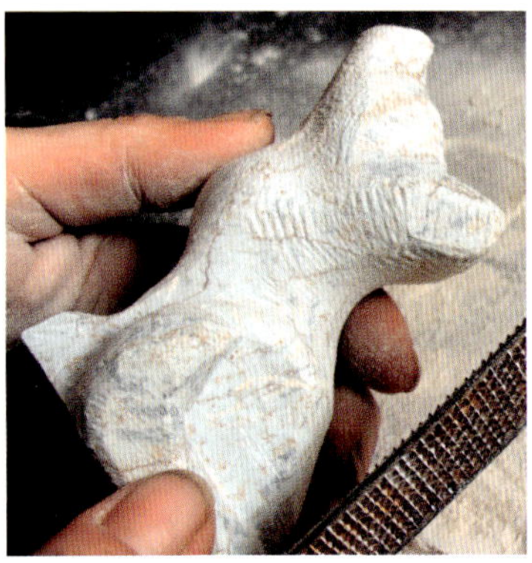

Using the file, begin rounding the chest. A gentle upward motion is the best choice for this area. Once again, it is important that your grip on the piece provides good support for the head, especially when working on the details of the muzzle and ears. Hold the file softly and let the motion remove the stone, not pressure. Repetition will yield the shape and softness. Look at the piece from the front and notice the lines. Using the curved side of the file, remove the lines that remain, beginning with the lower end, then the upper. It does not take much to remove these lines, so go slowly. Now begin generally rounding the coyote. Step back frequently to determine where you need to focus.

Continue rounding. Again, hold the file softly and let the motion remove the stone, not pressure. Take a step back and notice the shape emerging. Now there is only one flat area on the back and the centerline is right in the middle as the stone has been properly removed from both sides.

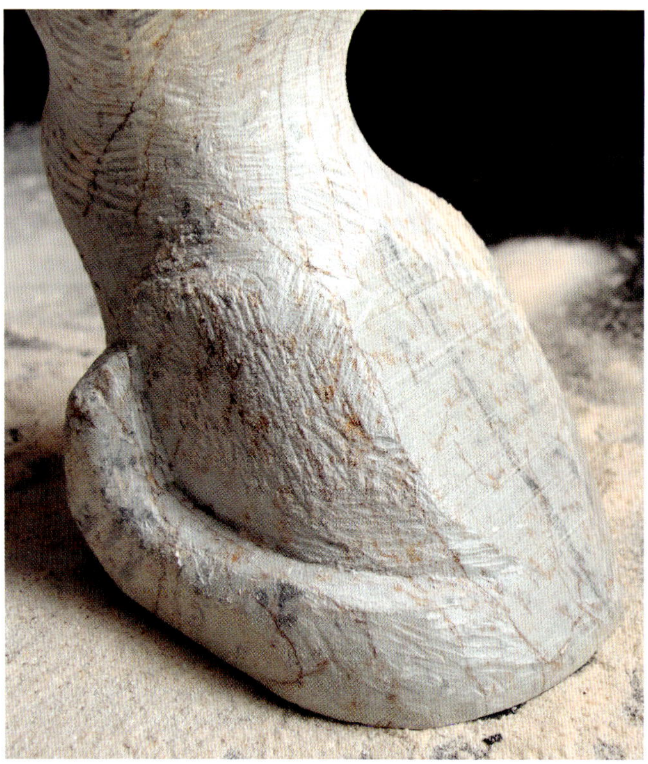

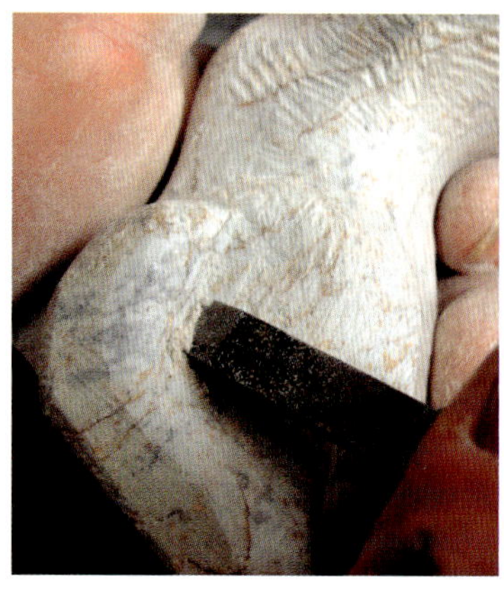

At this stage, you begin to critique your sculpture and can choose to add small details, such as a deeper tail line. The flat side of the chisel works well in these small areas. Add more definition to the tail.

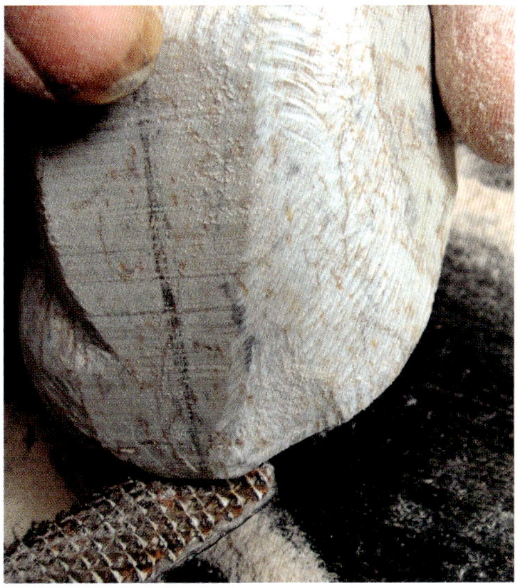

We want to give more definition to the back side of our coyote. Place the file to the right of the centerline on the back, curved side down and create a notch. The notch is not too deep.

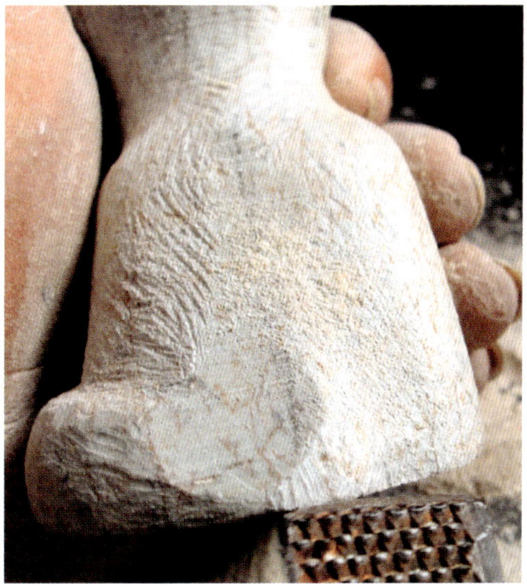

Continue rounding the body, starting with the back, working on the side, the shoulders, the base of the piece, returning to the back on the centerline, and delicately rounding the flat panel on the back. You will see the flat part slowly disappears as you gently work from the outside in.

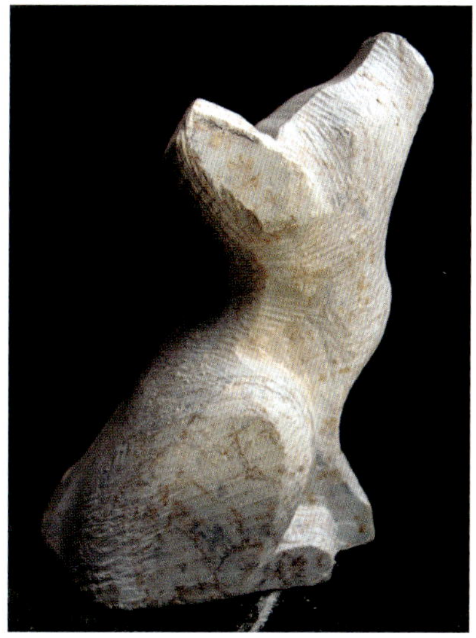

Take a look at your piece. Make sure it is even on both sides. Here is the side view. Inspect all of the features, including the back, head, muzzle, ears, paws, and tail. It is always good to look at your piece from all angles.

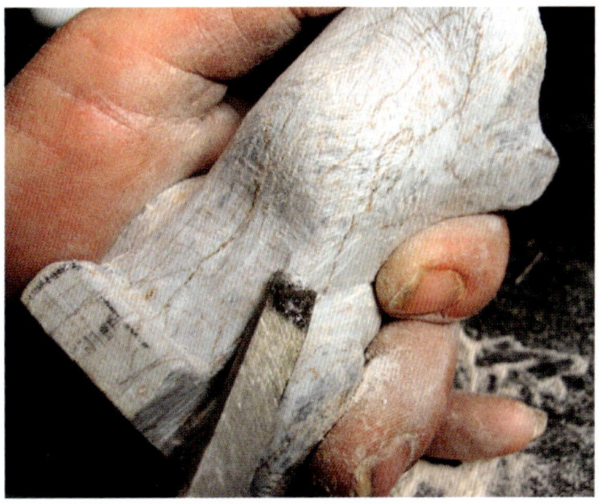

After looking at the piece we have found areas that still need some work. The chest area could use some additional smoothing and definition. Also touch up the paw line with the chisel. Add a bit more definition. Chisel to the desired depth. Each side could use some evening to match the other. In an upward sweeping motion, use the chisel to remove stone from the legs and define the chest area. This is subtle but effective. Start at the base and sweep up.

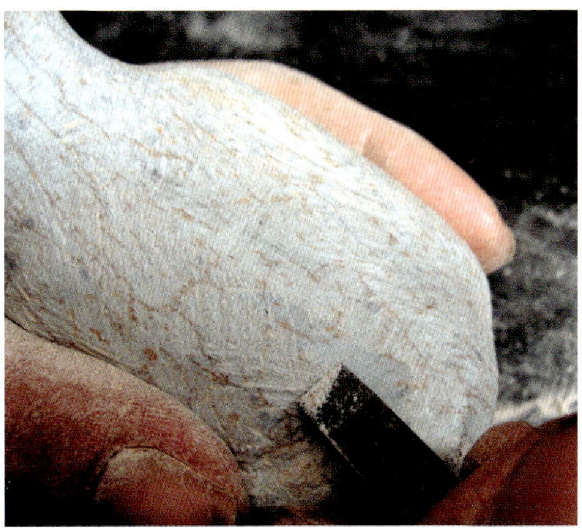

Remove small imperfections: The chisel is good for smoothing the stone on the paws by the leg, the base of the tail, and the flat panel on the back. Use a good grip with slow movement to gently remove the stone.

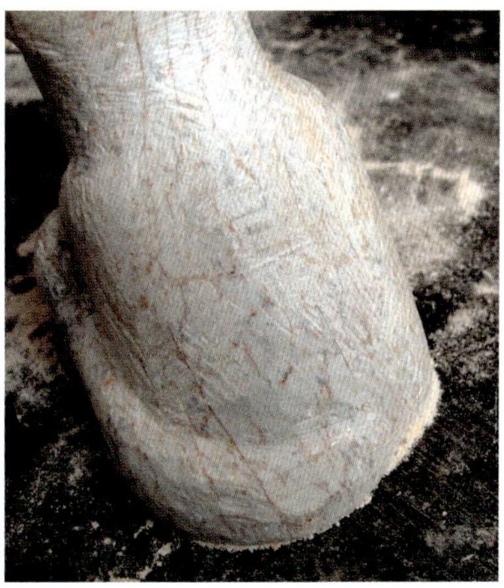

Continue until you have completed the back area, working to the centerline. This is how your piece should look at this stage.

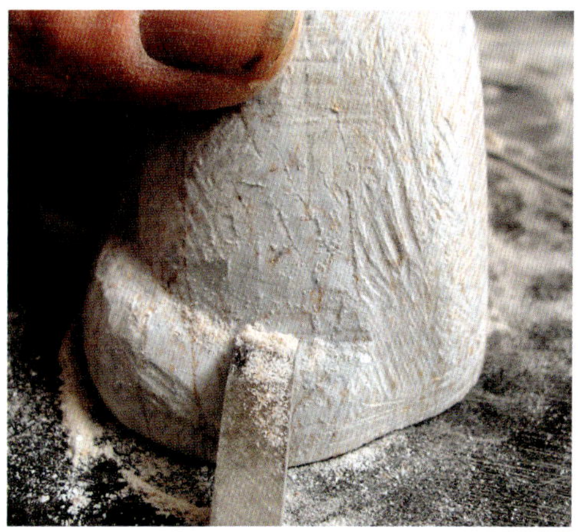

In order to eventuate the tail, we need to redefine the line of the tail to the centerline of the back. Bring the line all the way to the area where we created the notch earlier. Work the area where the tail meets the back and deepen the line.

Detailing the Head

Here we focus on detailing the head of the coyote. In order to shape the face, carve the ears, and define the eyes and muzzle, you must work slowly and have a lot of patience. We will be utilizing the chisel, the four-sided file, a pencil, and a rasp.

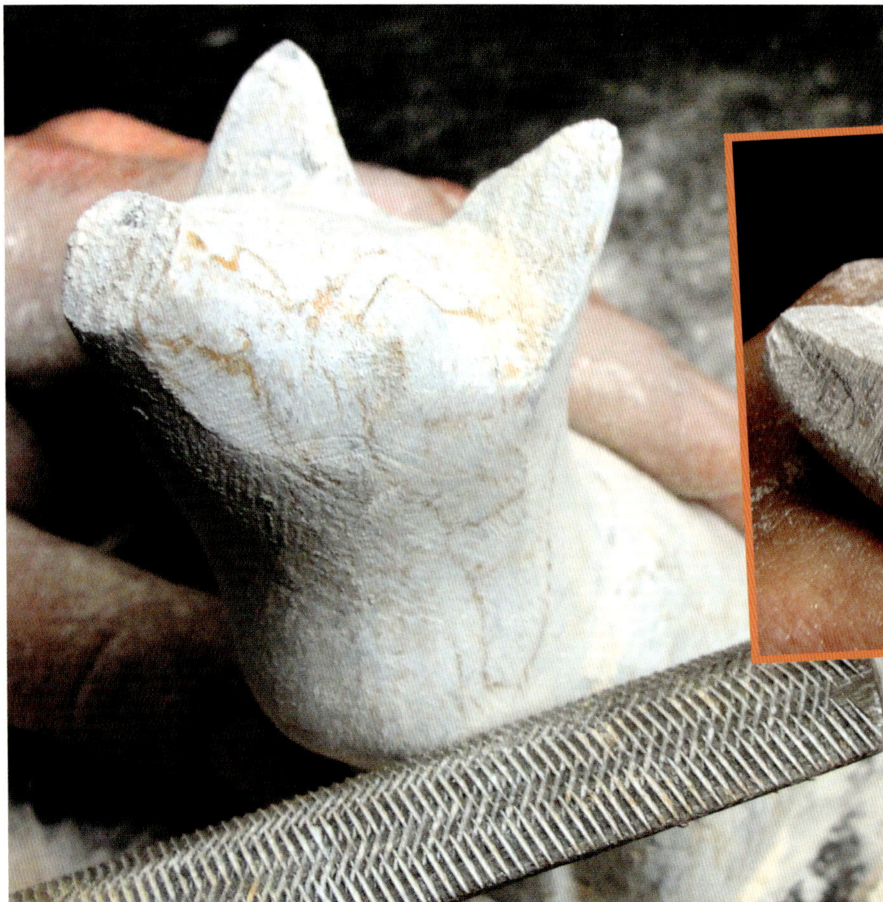

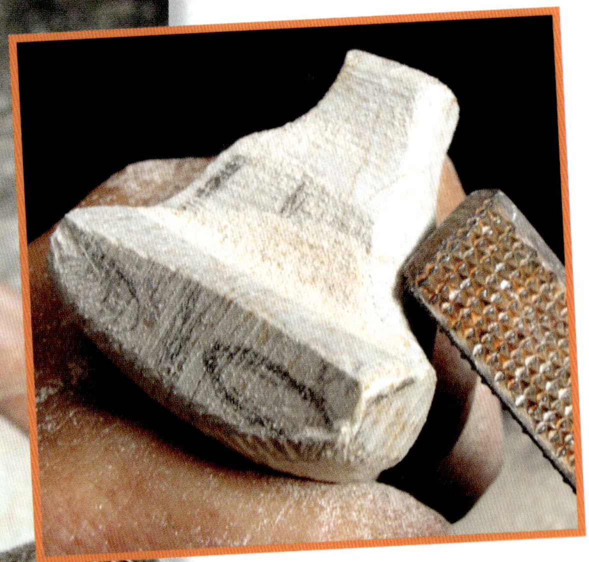

Before filing, make sure that your grip on the piece is such that the head is always supported. Look at the lines on the top and sides of the muzzle. We will be shaping the muzzle by smoothing the angles of the stone to the line of the muzzle with the rounded side of the file. In an upward motion to the left, gently file the muzzle. Remember to let the motion remove the stone and not pressure. Repeat on the other side.

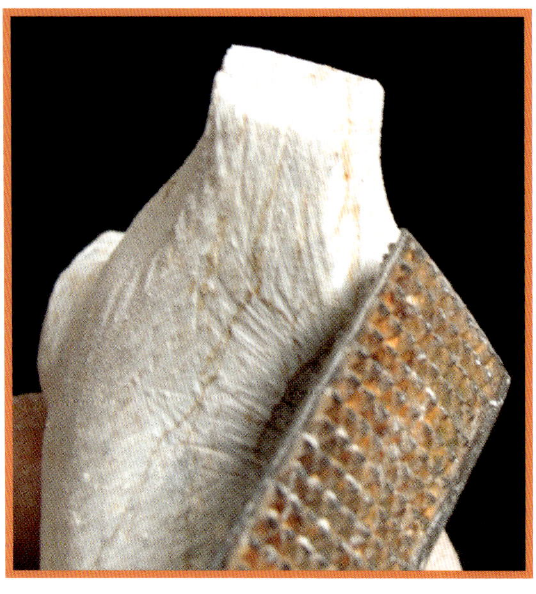

Contour the jaw from below using the same rounding technique.

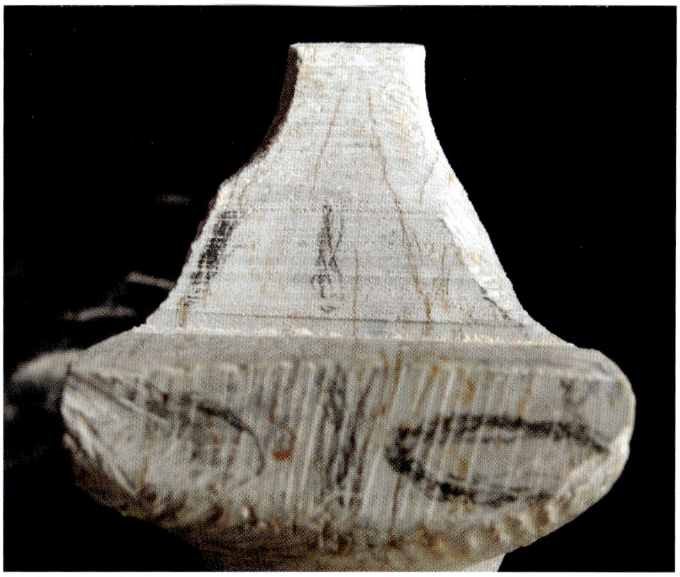

You should see the hard lines fade away. View from the top. Look at the symmetry of the piece. Check each side. When working on this level of detail, it is important to check the centerline often.

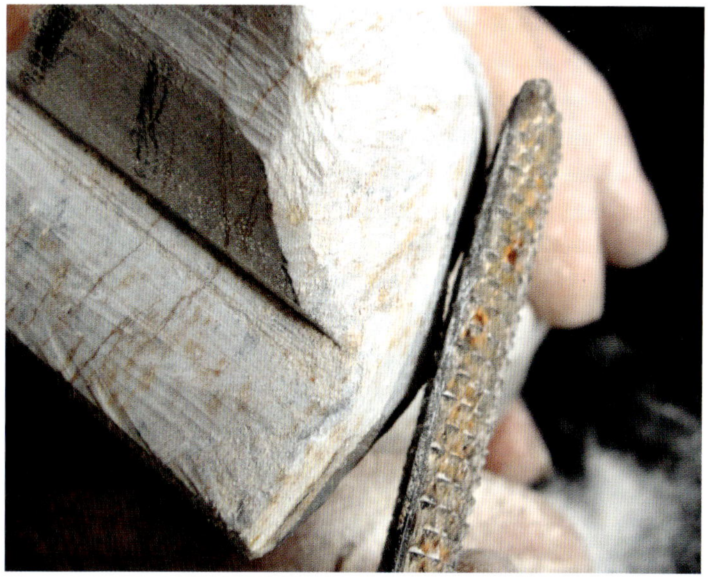

Begin on the right ear, in an downward motion, smoothing the stone. The jaw begins to round with the motion not pressure. Remember your grip.

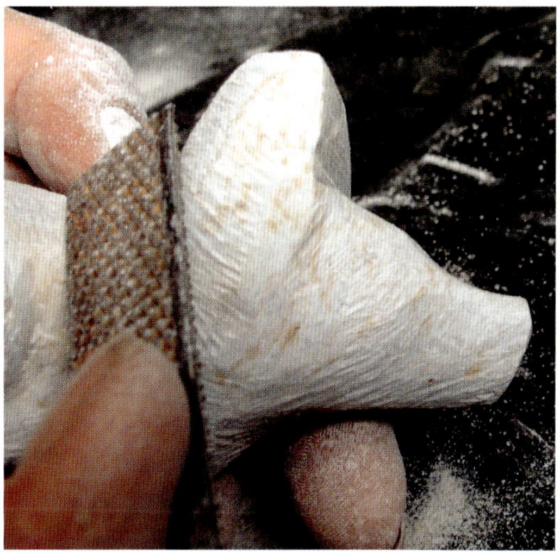

Begin working behind the ear. Again, slowly. Repeat on the other side.

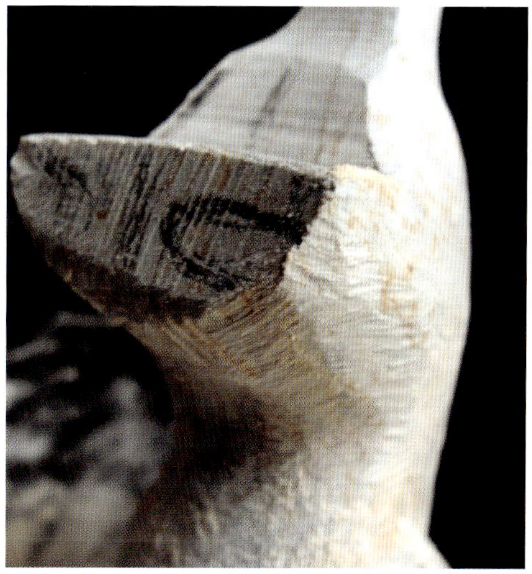

Notice how the back of the ears are rounded.

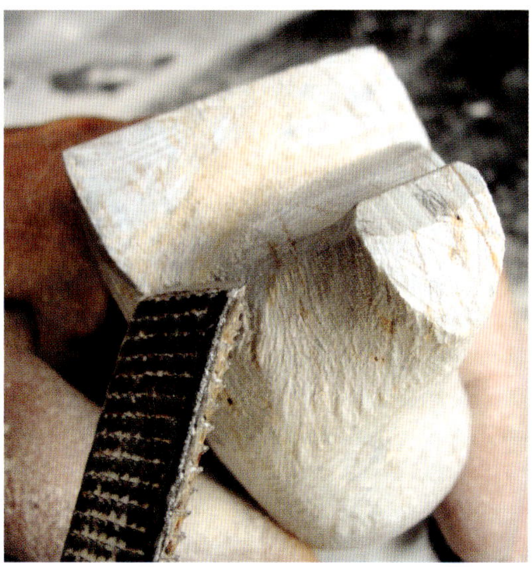

Using the file, focus on rounding the edge of the muzzle to make the angles fade. Again work very slowly. Only file at an angle as to not remove the top material. Repeat on the other side.

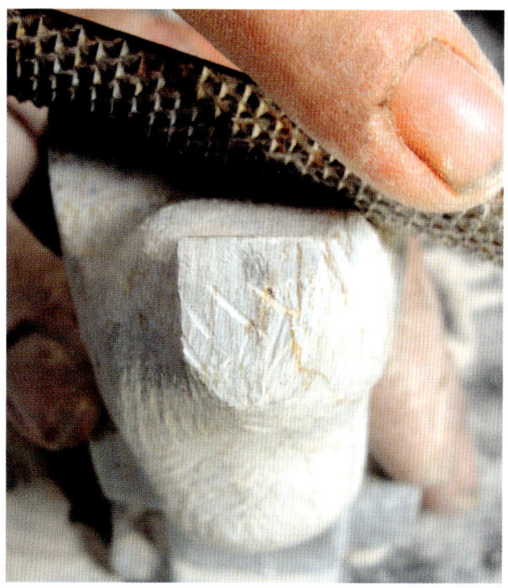

Look at the piece from the front and begin shaping the eye area with the file. Start by gently moving up, over the ridge of the brow, and then down the other side.

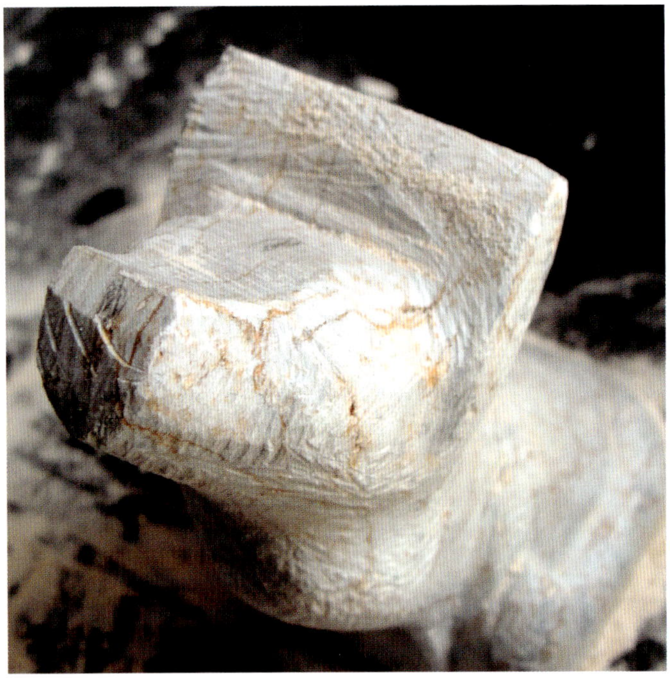

Continue rounding until your piece looks something like this.

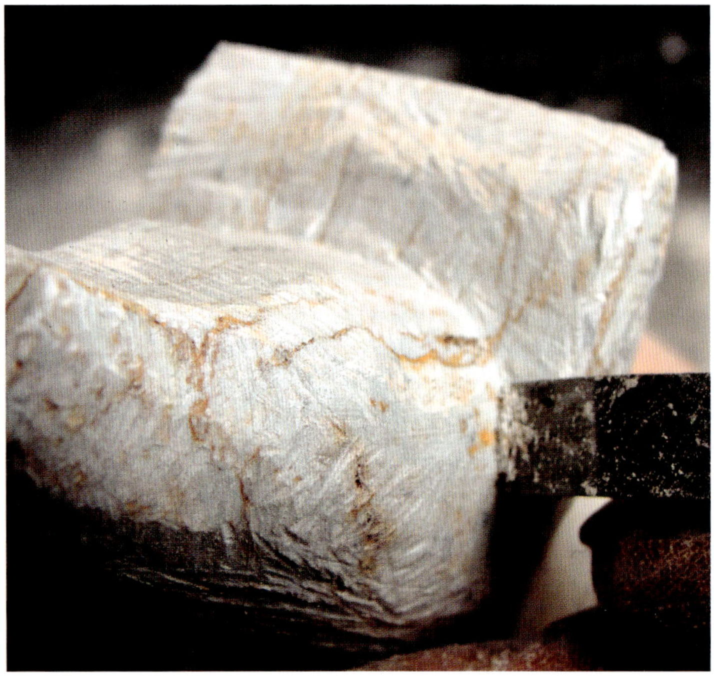

Now with the chisel, you will work on adding definition to the face by removing material above the base of the ears. The flat side of the chisel starts at the base and scrapes up to remove material. Once again don't dig too deep, don't apply too much pressure, take it slow. You can hardly see the chisel marks. Go over the area repeatedly.

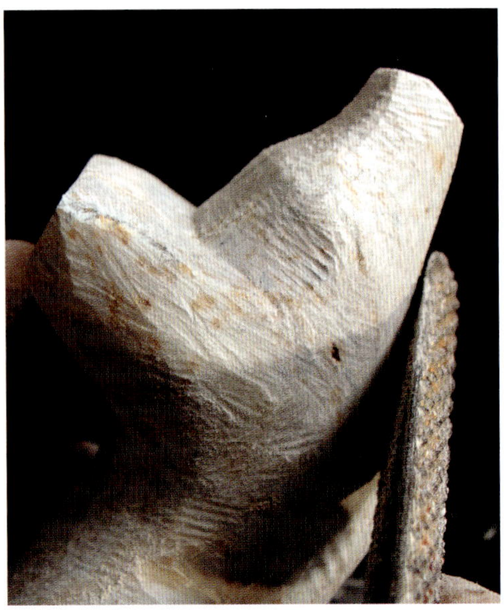

Take a break from the chisel and study the piece. Here we are smoothing out the jaw line.

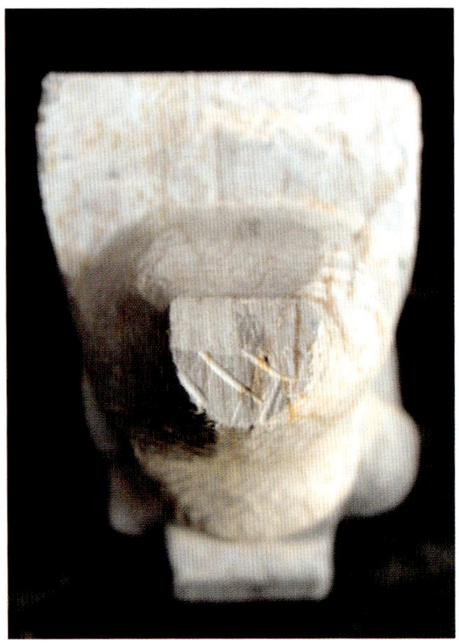

Here is a view from the top, notice the centerline and the general symmetry of the piece.

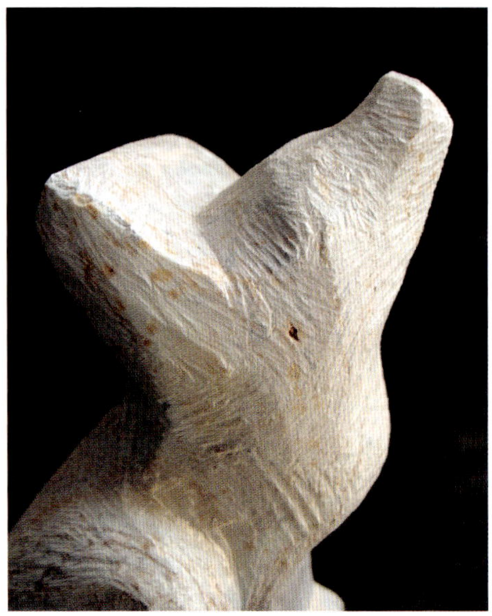

Side view.

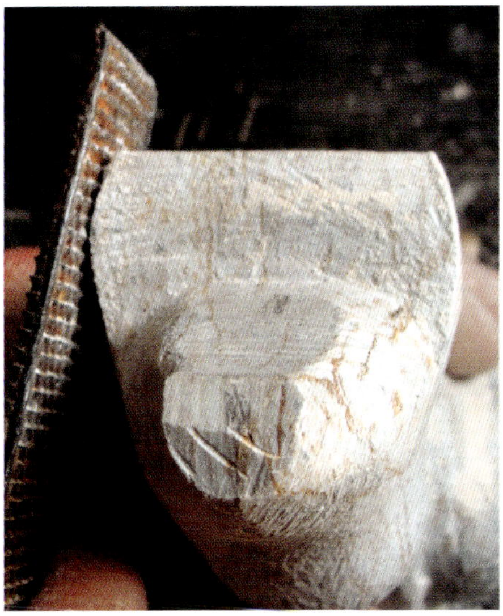

At this point you will tackle the ears. Remember your grip, let the tool do the work, not pressure. You are working on shaping the delicate tips of the ears. Repeat on both sides. Notice how even the muzzle is and how the jaw line and ears are even on both sides. Add a little more angle to the tip of the ear on both sides.

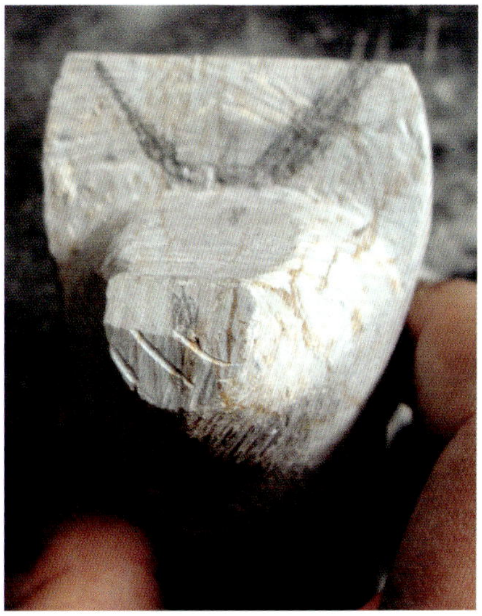

You can now pick up your pencil and begin drawing back the lines that will be your ears. Starting at the centerline, moving up and out. Go over the line again. Have a pencil sharpener handy, just in case. Make sure your line is nice and dark. Repeat on the other side. Look at the piece. You should have equal material on both sides to form the ears.

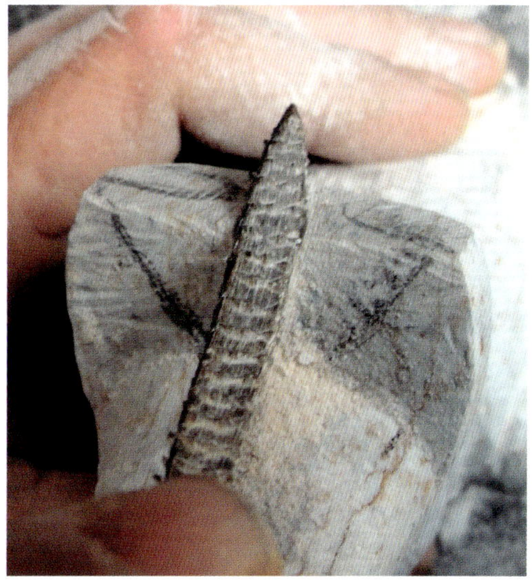

Pick up the rasp and go to your centerline. Begin filing gently on the centerline between the ears.

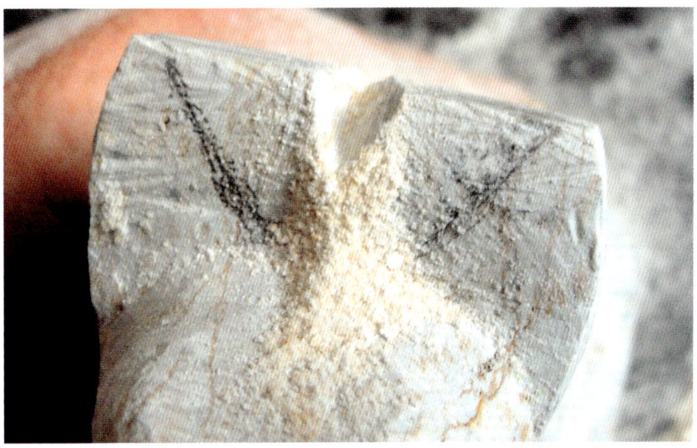

You should see a slight V in just a few strokes.

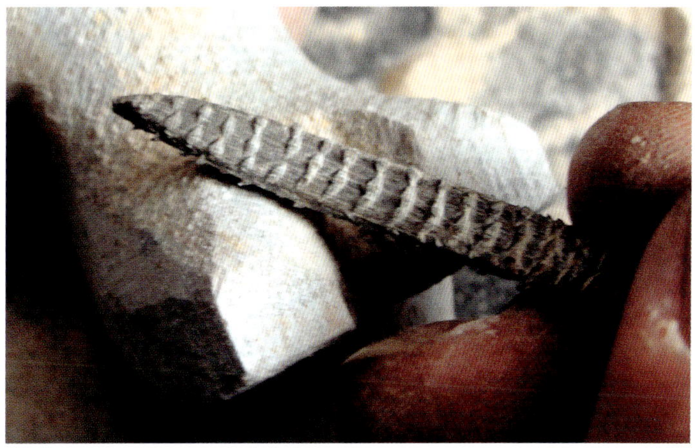

Clean off the piece and continue to remove the stone. Again, go slow and let the tool do the work, do not apply heavy pressure. It is better to take more time than to risk breaking an ear. Now once the indentation has been created to the desired depth, begin rotating the rasp and shaping the ears. Repeat on the front. Remember your grasp. Go slowly and gently, widening the space between the ears following the lines. At this stage you can begin shaping the back of the ear.

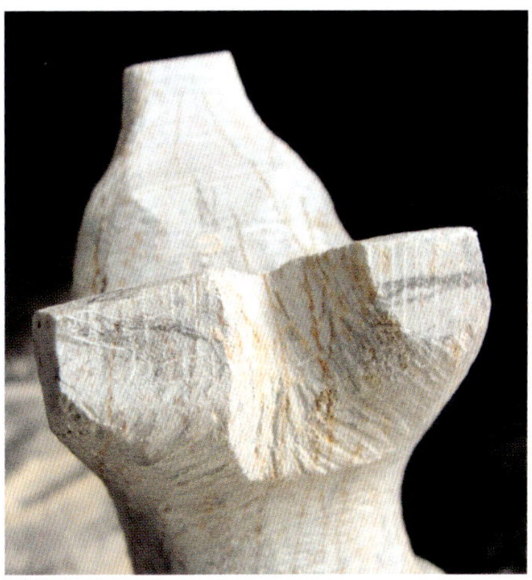

Here you can see the difference between the ears.

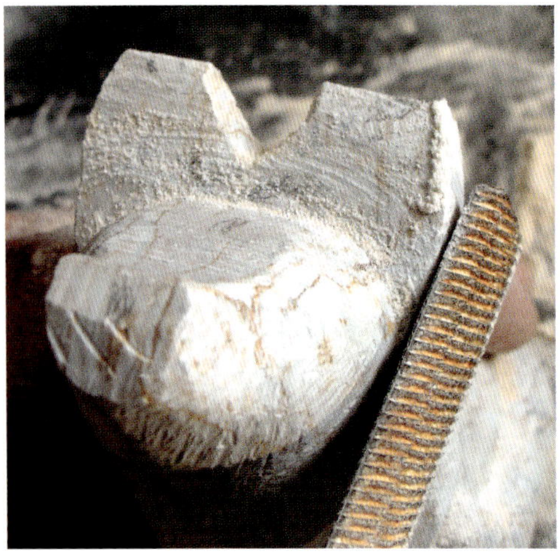

View from the front. Notice how we did not go too deep, too fast. With your file, flatten the front of the ears using a sweeping motion. Then take a look at your piece.

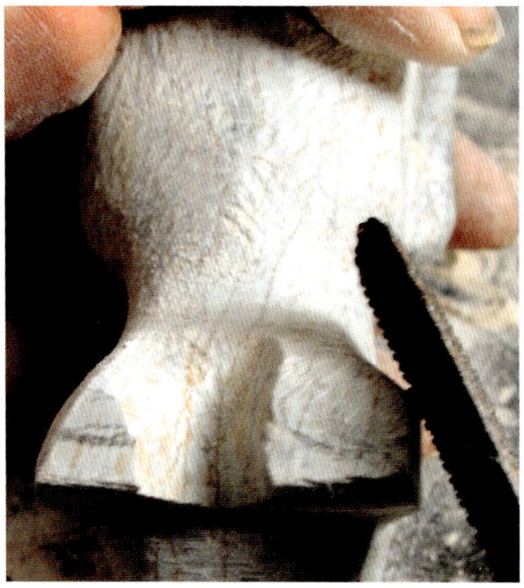

Using the file, begin to round the ear with extreme care. Remember the grip and let the tool do the work, not pressure! Work on the back of the ear. Here is a view from the top. Use the flat side of the file to shape your ears.

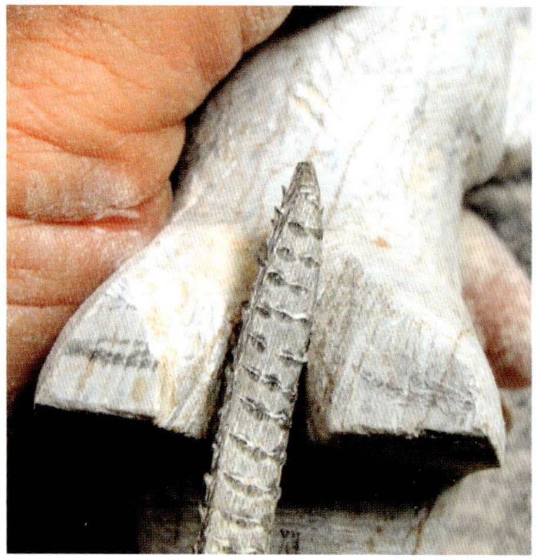

Pick up your rasp and continue refining. Now that material has been removed from both sides of the ears you can deepen the crevice that separates them.

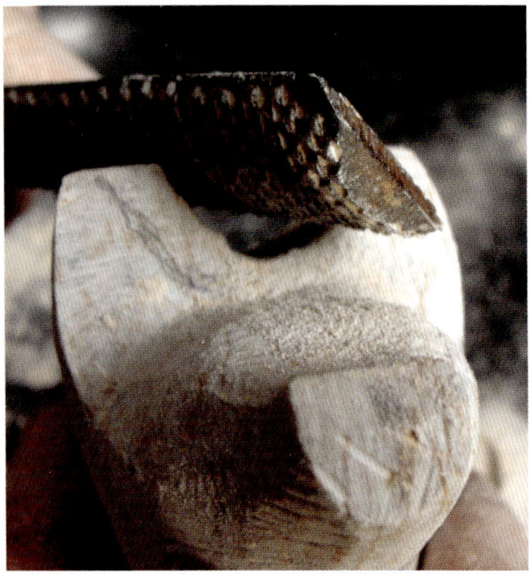

Once again, referring to the centerline, redraw the ears so that they will be even. Repeat on both sides. Take the round side of the file and begin eliminating material, working towards your ear line. The file creates a natural curve forming the ear. Repeat on the other side.

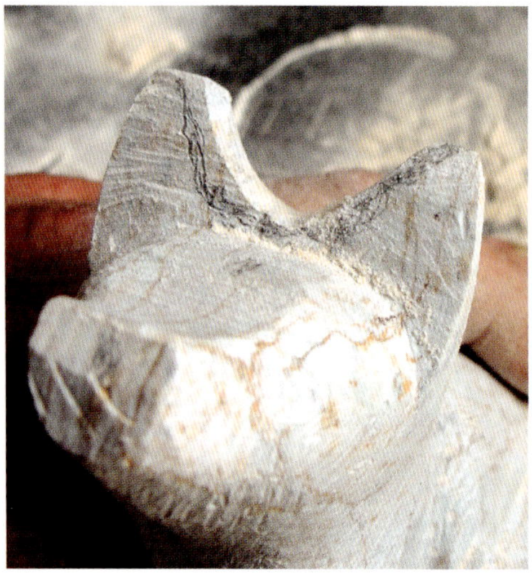

Stop and take a look to see how even your ears are.

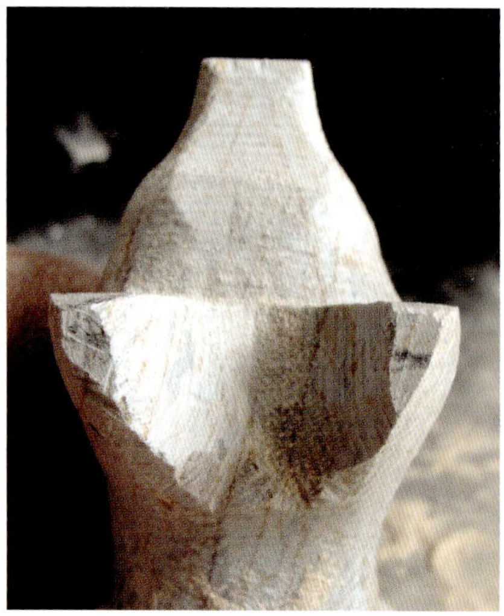

View from the top.

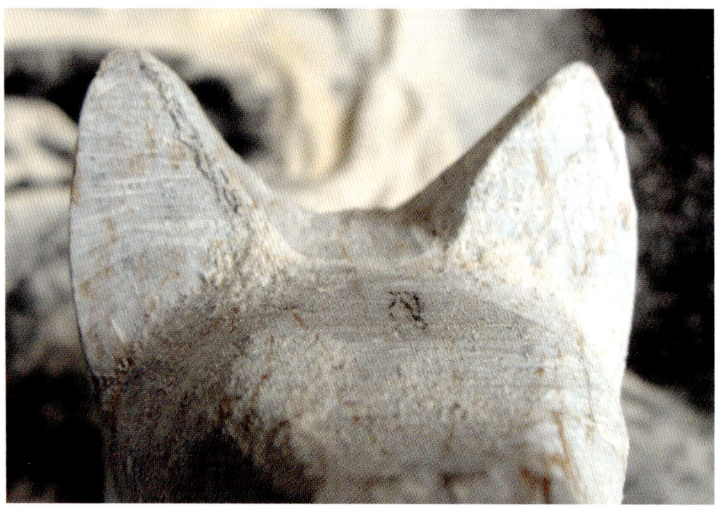

Continue to shape the ears. Work slowly, on one side then the other. Carefully work around the lines. The centerline is still apparent on the muzzle and the evenness of the ears is apparent. The chisel is the best tool to use to finish this task as you get close to the guide lines. Notice how evenly shaped the muzzle and the ears are to the centerline now, even though we did not go all the way to the pencil line.

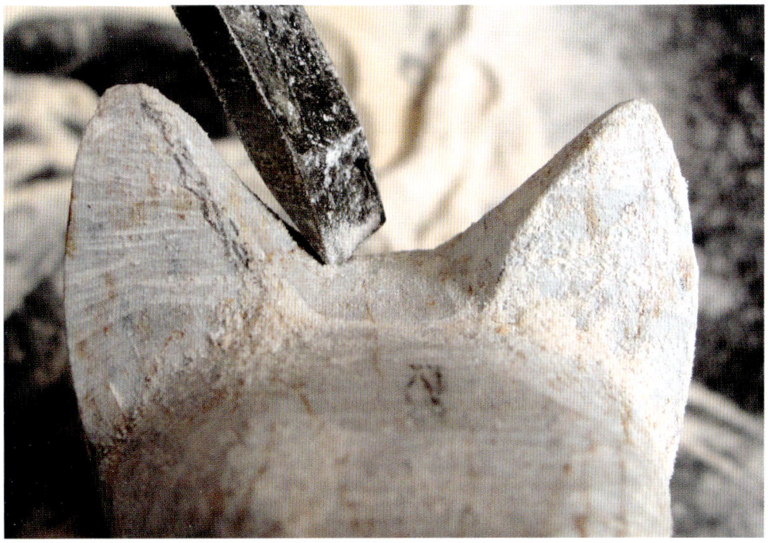

With the chisel, define the base of the ears.

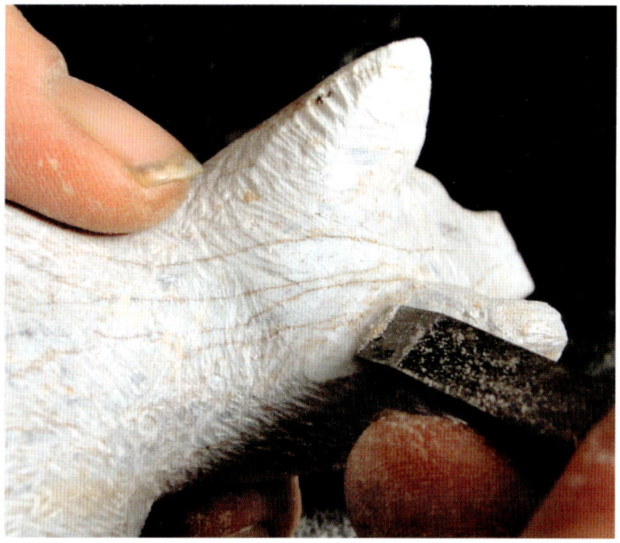

Follow the lines behind the ears with the tip of the chisel.

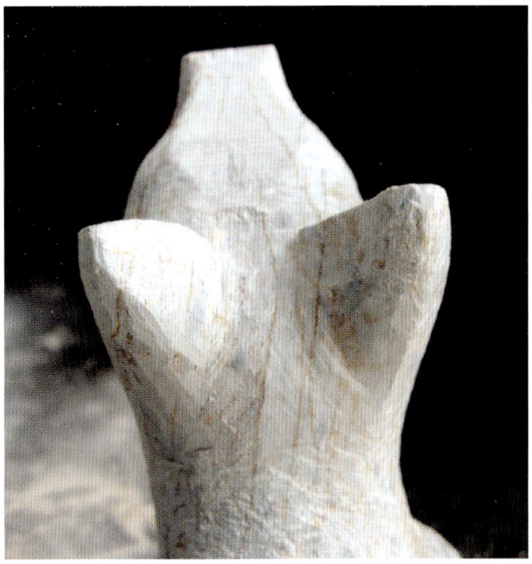

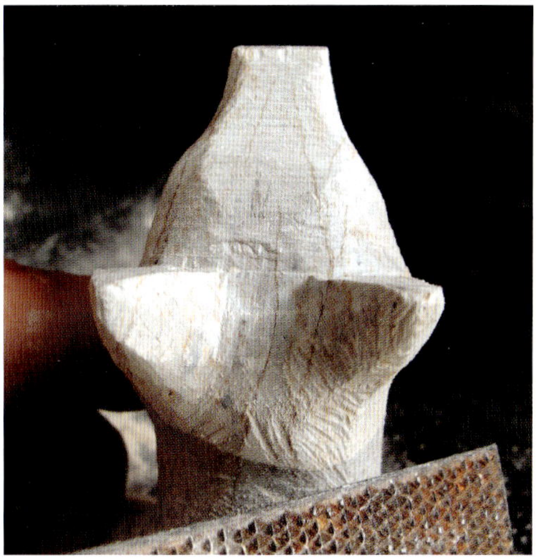

With the flat file, rounded side down, begin refining the back of the ear. Work gently and slowly, remember the grip, allow the tool to do the work, not the pressure. You are just moving the file in an upward motion to remove material and make a thinner ear. In just a few strokes, notice how the difference in the thickness. Be sure to go around to the side. Again, notice from this angle the difference in thickness.

Back view: Notice here you can see the light chisel marks.

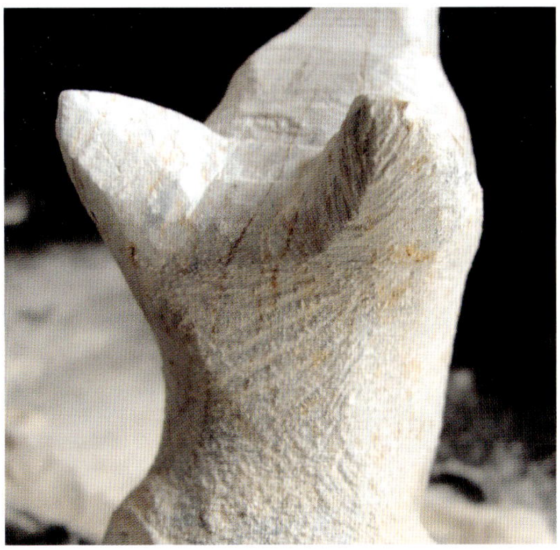

The file marks seem to be prominent, but do not worry, they will be removed.

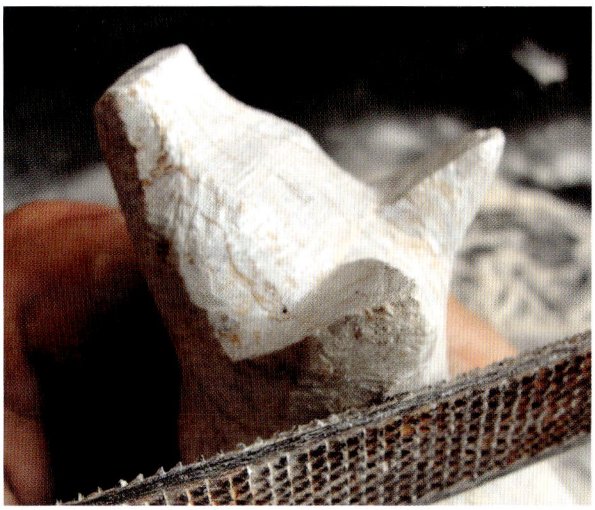

Continue rounding on the other side, using a gentle rounding motion.

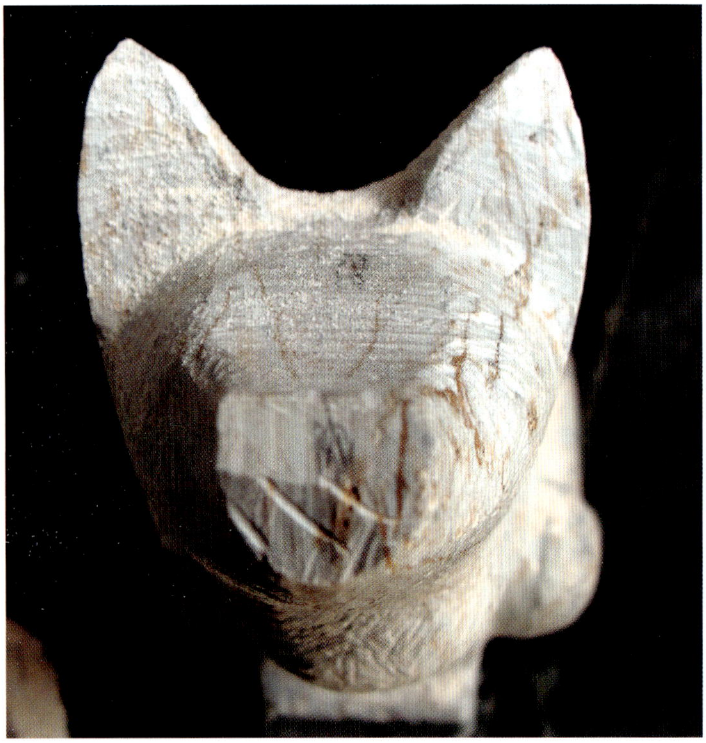

The ears still need some work. Focus on the inside of the ear. Stop frequently and take a look at the piece so that you don't remove too much material. Front view: Now you can really see how evenly balanced the ears are now.

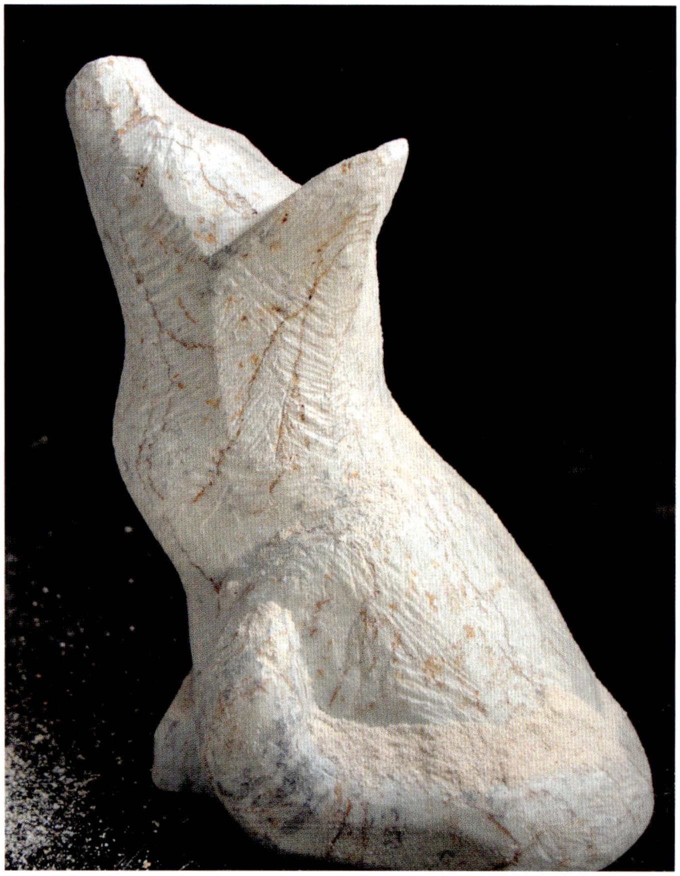

Side view. Notice both how much thinner the ears are and the detail at the ear tips.

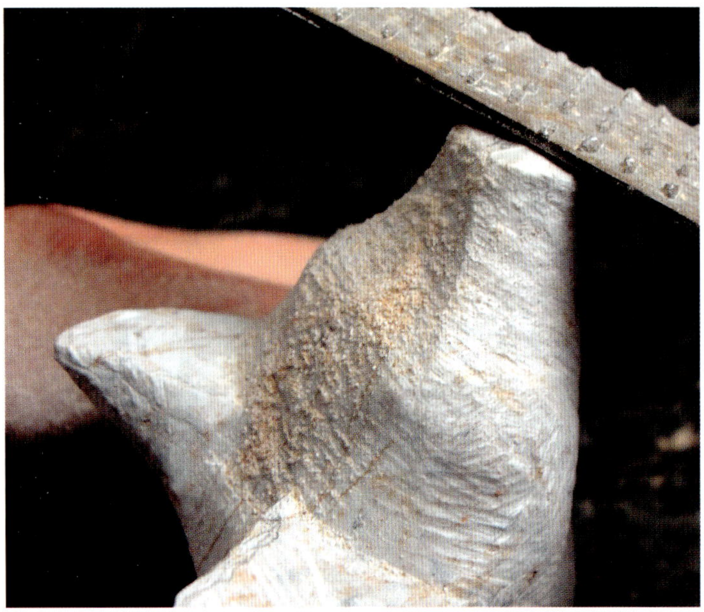

In looking at the piece we noticed that the muzzle needed some touching up. Touching up the other side. Touch up the tip of the muzzle, smoothing out the nose with the finer side of the file.

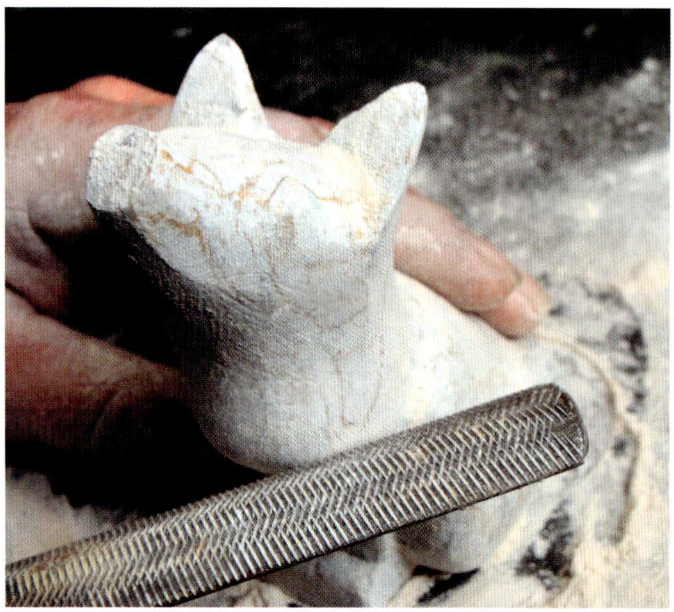

The fine side of the file is used to smooth out the file marks.
File the entire piece to remove deep marks. Notice the muzzle is now more delicate and the texture of the stone is much smoother. Close up of the head; at this stage the head should look something like this.

3 Finishing and Polishing

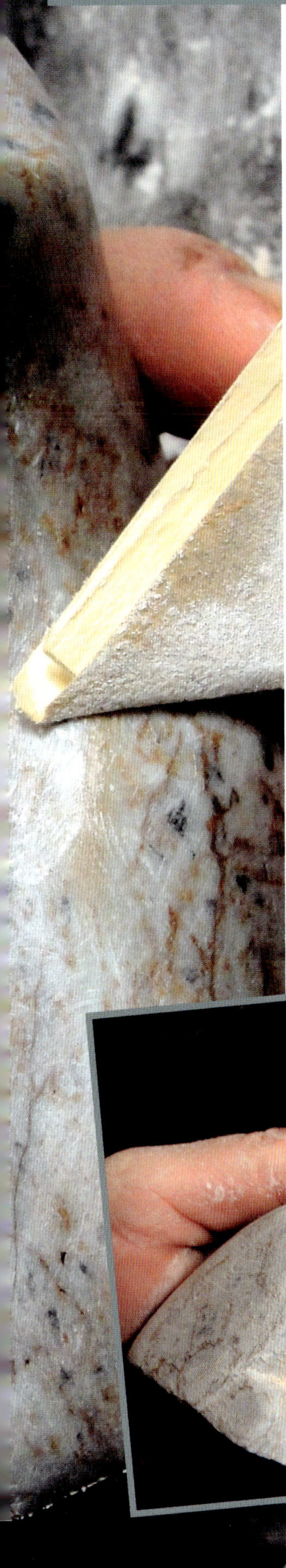

Here you will be sanding, finishing, and polishing the coyote. This is the final stage of your project and you will need a small file, sandpapers, and some lacquer finish (or whatever you wish to use to polish your piece).

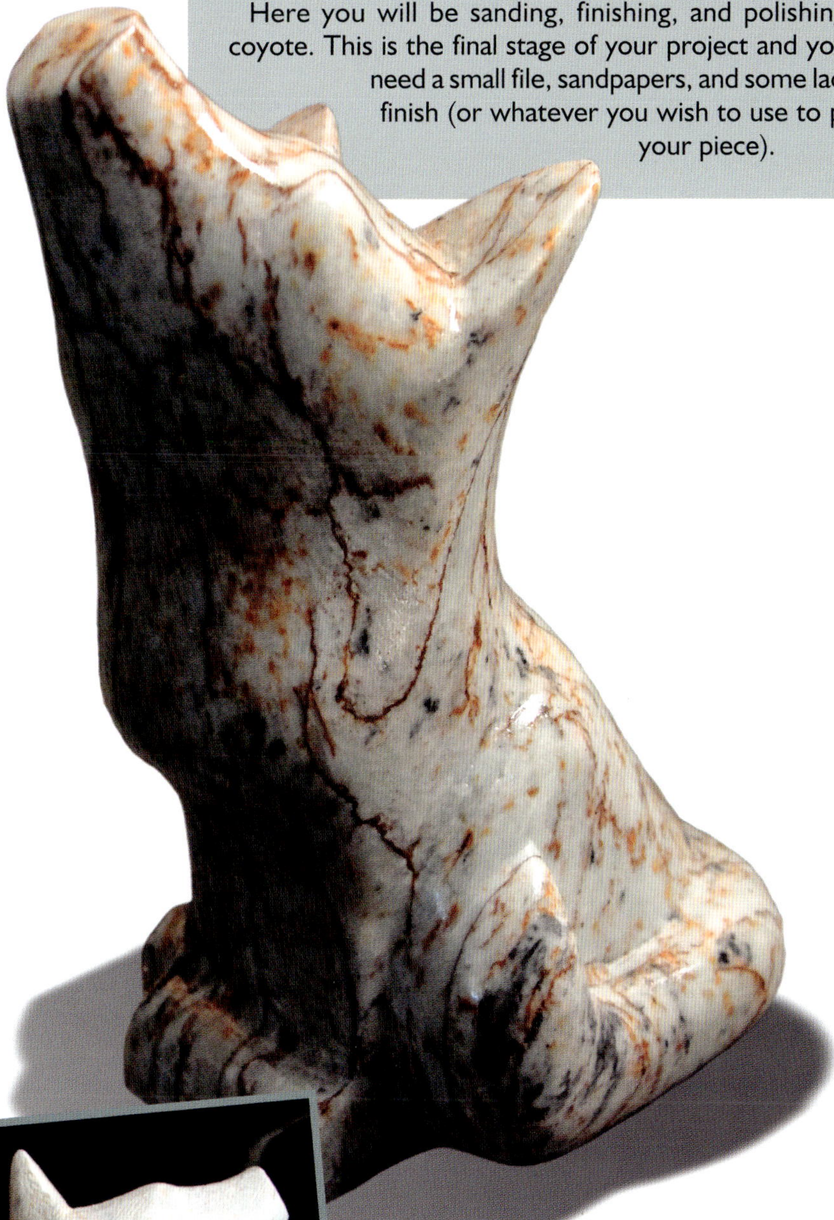

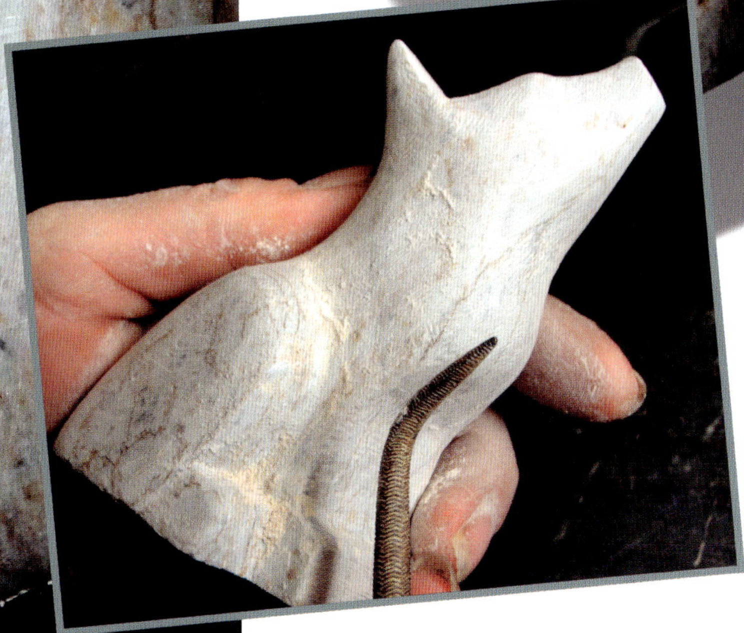

We chose to use a curved needle file to remove the small file marks that still remained because the curve of the file contours the curves of the coyote well. However, if you can not find a needle file, you can use sandpapers.

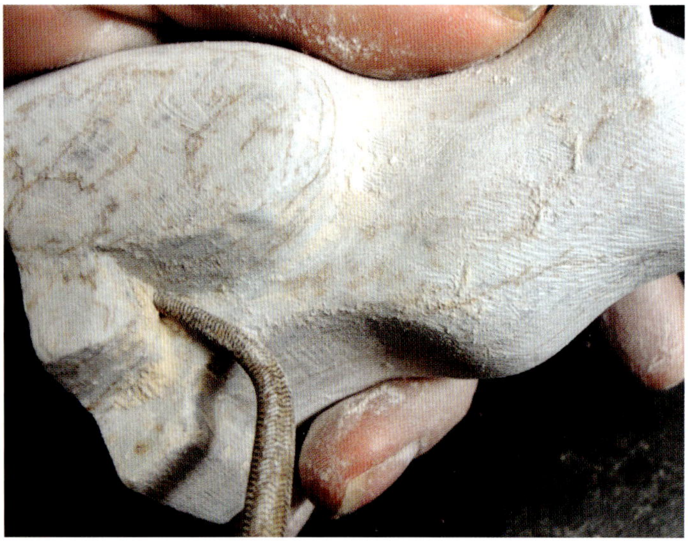

Smoothing the crease in the leg. Smooth the entire piece.

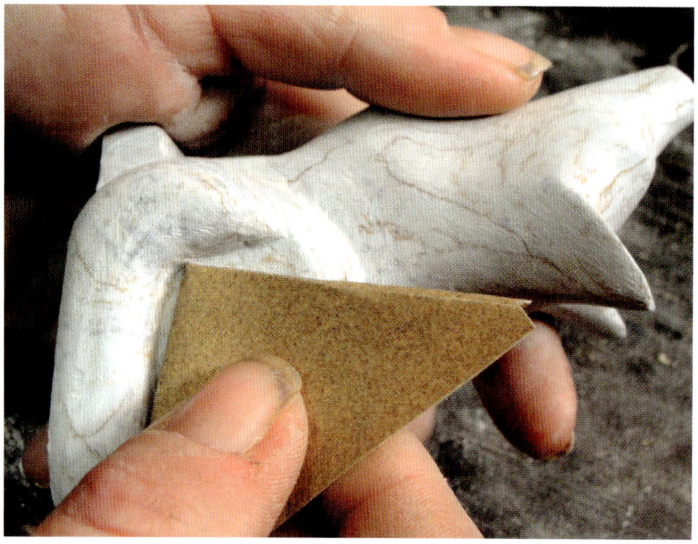

Once the file marks have been removed to your satisfaction with the file, take some sandpaper and fold it. Starting with 80 grit, then 120, then 220, begin working in the creases with the corner of the sandpaper. Sand all areas needing attention. Take a step back and look for any missed spots.

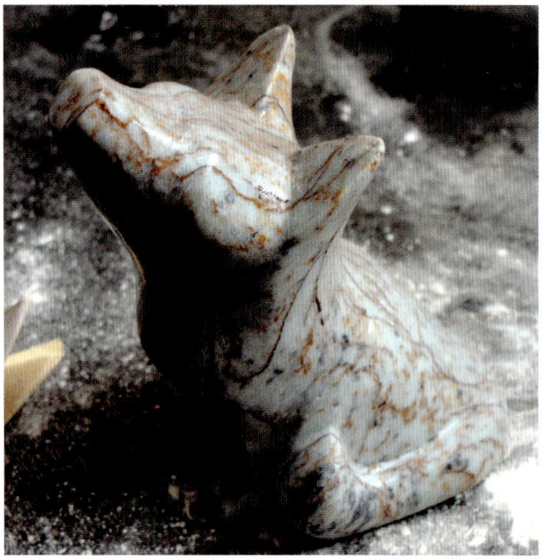

Wet the piece down with water to remove the fine dust. This will also allow you to see the areas, if any, that need more sanding.

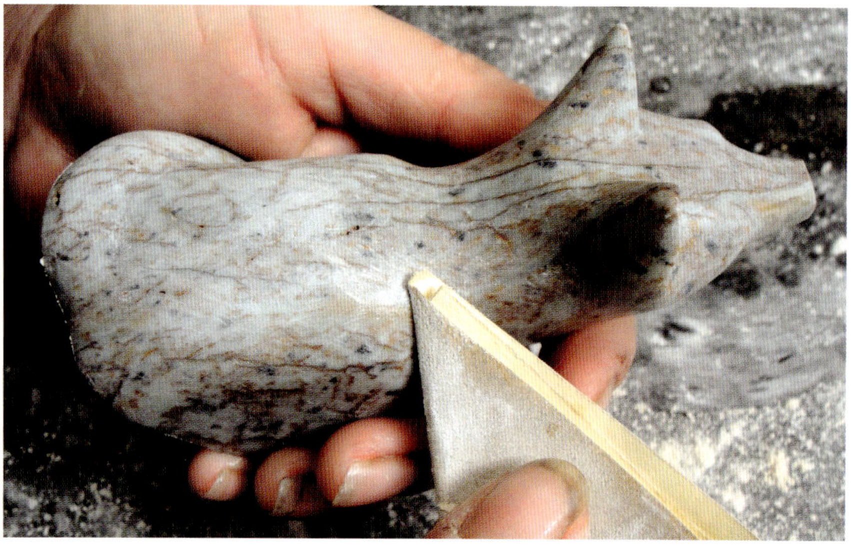

As you can see, there are file marks that still need to be removed. Leaving the piece wet, you can sand the marks off. (If you choose, you can use wet/dry sandpaper).

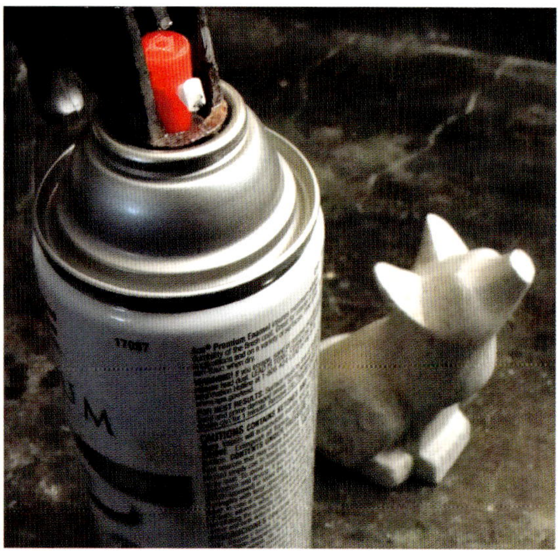

We chose to use clear spray enamel in a glossy finish.

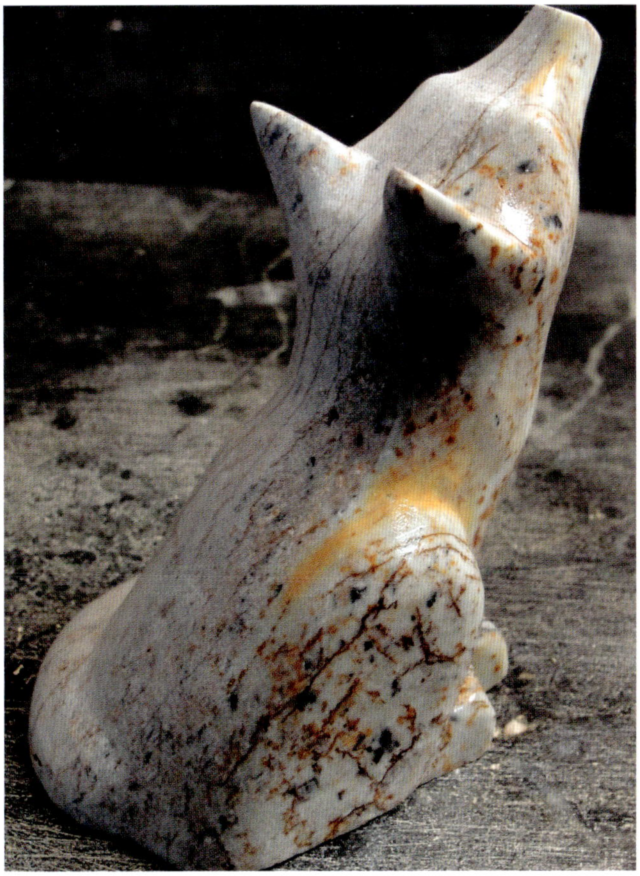

We recommend spraying the piece outdoors. Apply the finish in short, light bursts of spray in a sweeping motion from side to side. You do not want to apply too much spray at once. You can always repeat the spraying. Applying too much will cause run lines. Here you can see where the spray was applied as a first layer on one side.

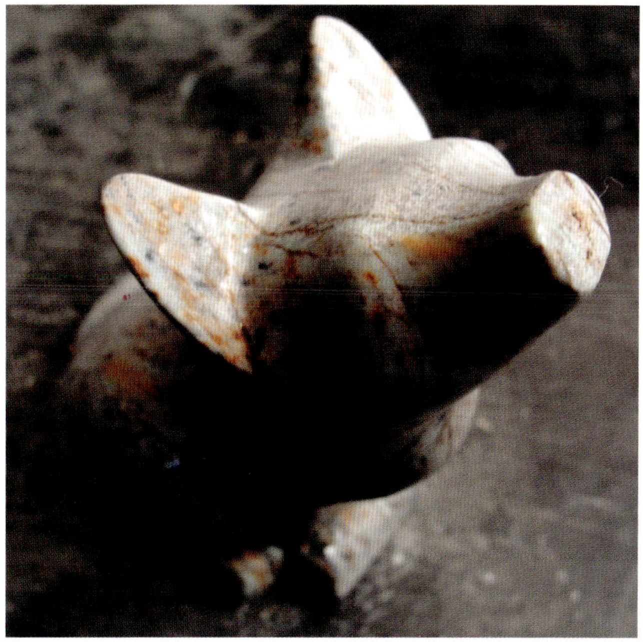

Notice how the colors pop out of the stone.

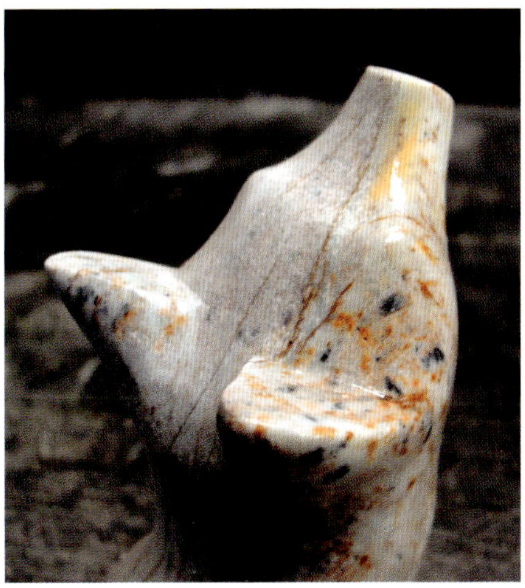

Top view.

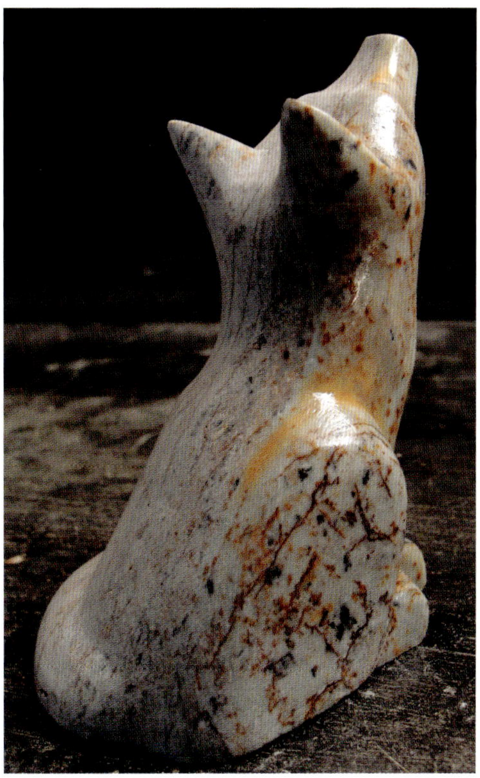

Back view, no drips.

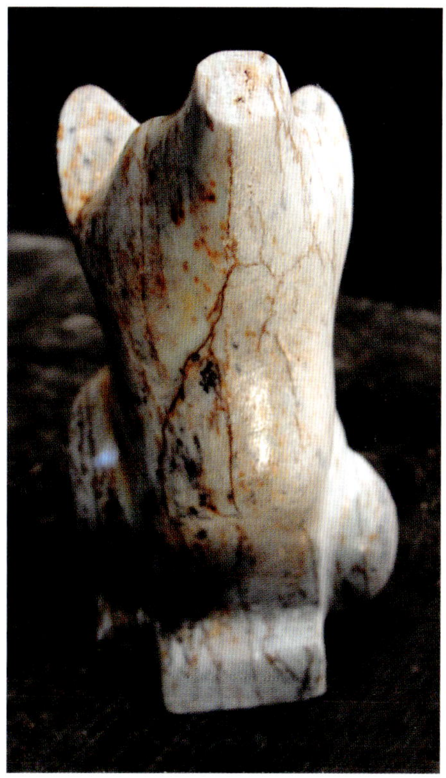

Front view, no drips.

Congratulations! You have completed your coyote!

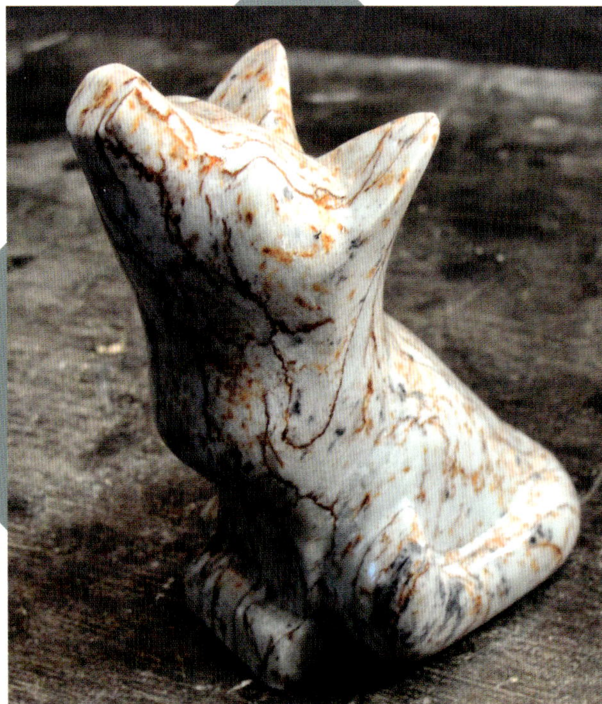

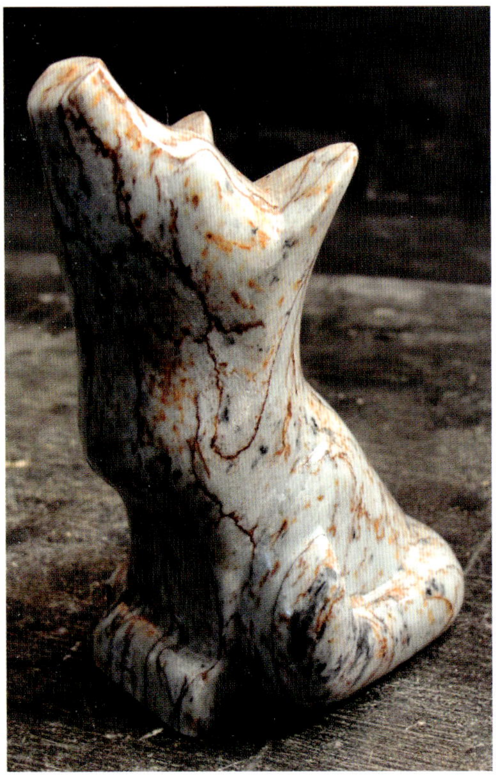

The coyote.

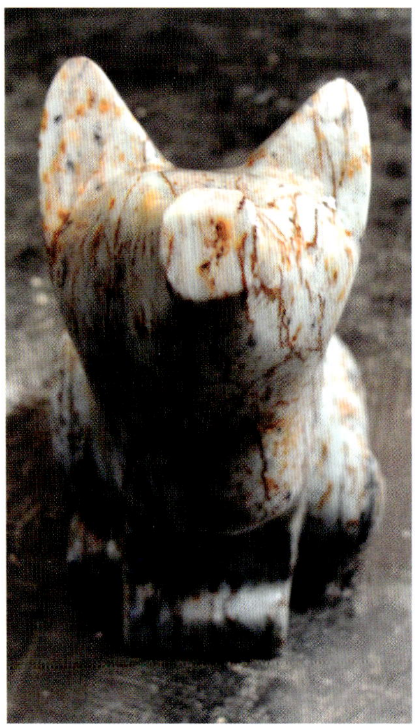

Top view.

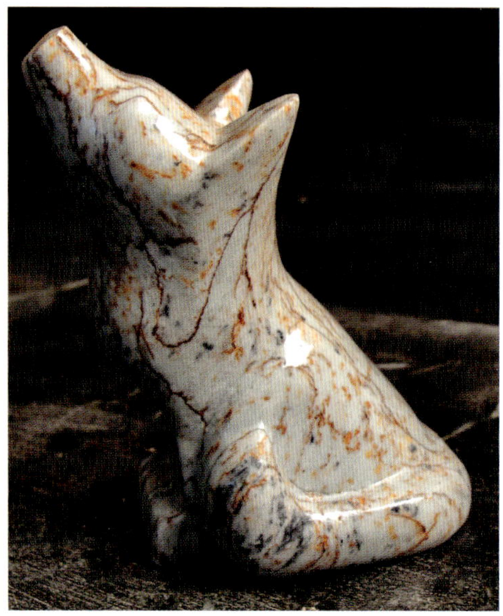

Tail side view.

Coyote Pattern

Patterns to use on a block or raw piece of soapstone. We recommend that you make copies of the patterns before cutting them out.

* Center line must lay 1/4" to either side of dead center to accommodate the tail, which is off centered.

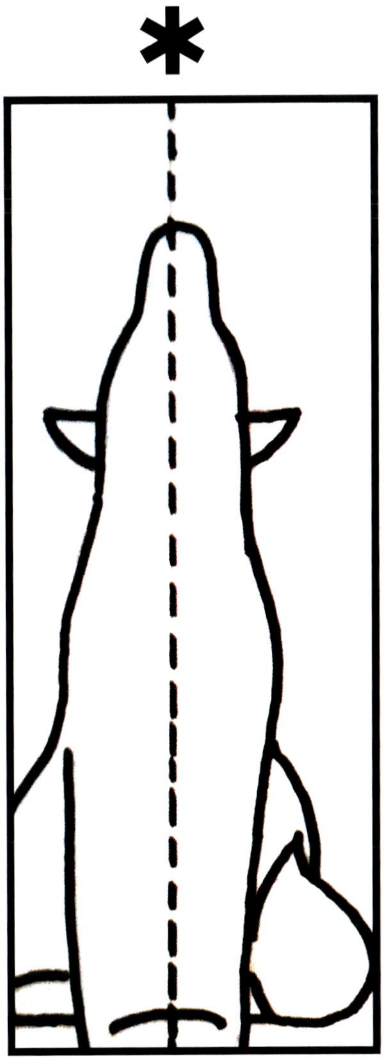

Front view

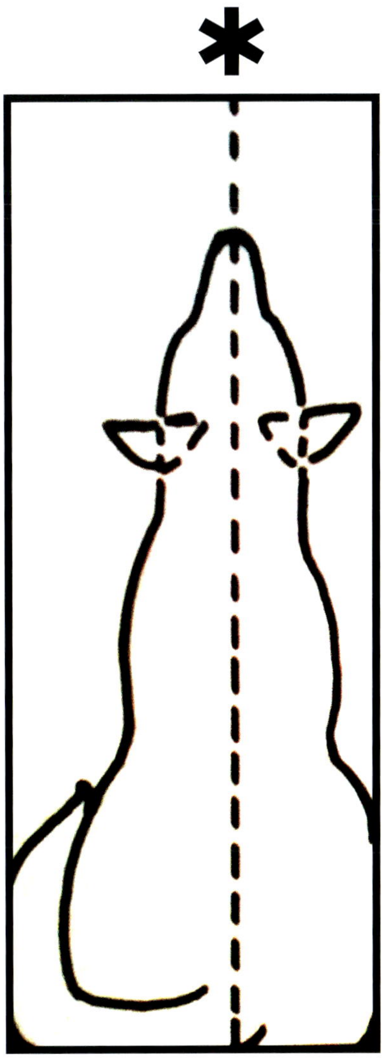

Back view

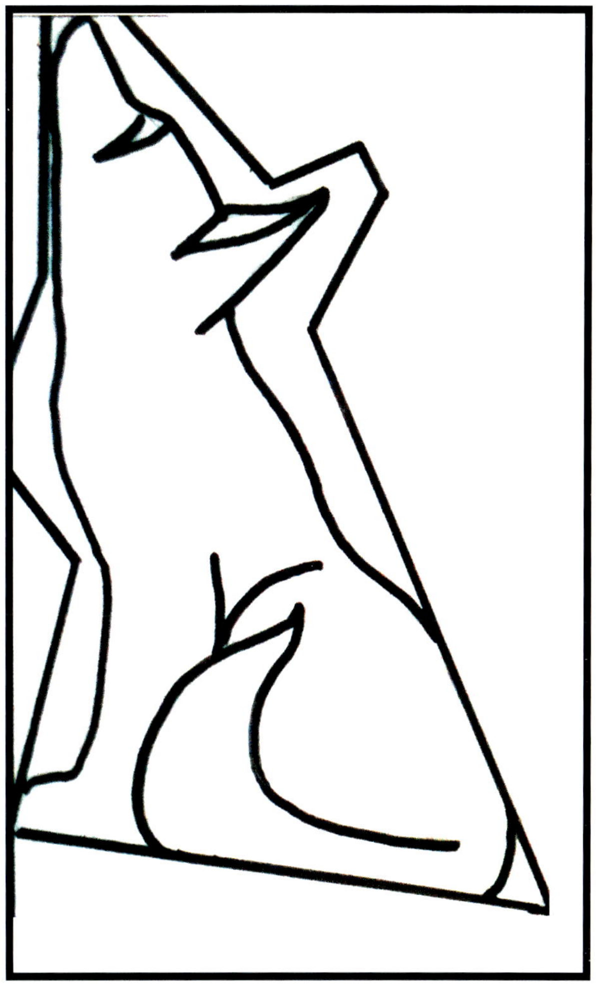

Side view

Gallery

Some examples of Dawn Hartwig's art.

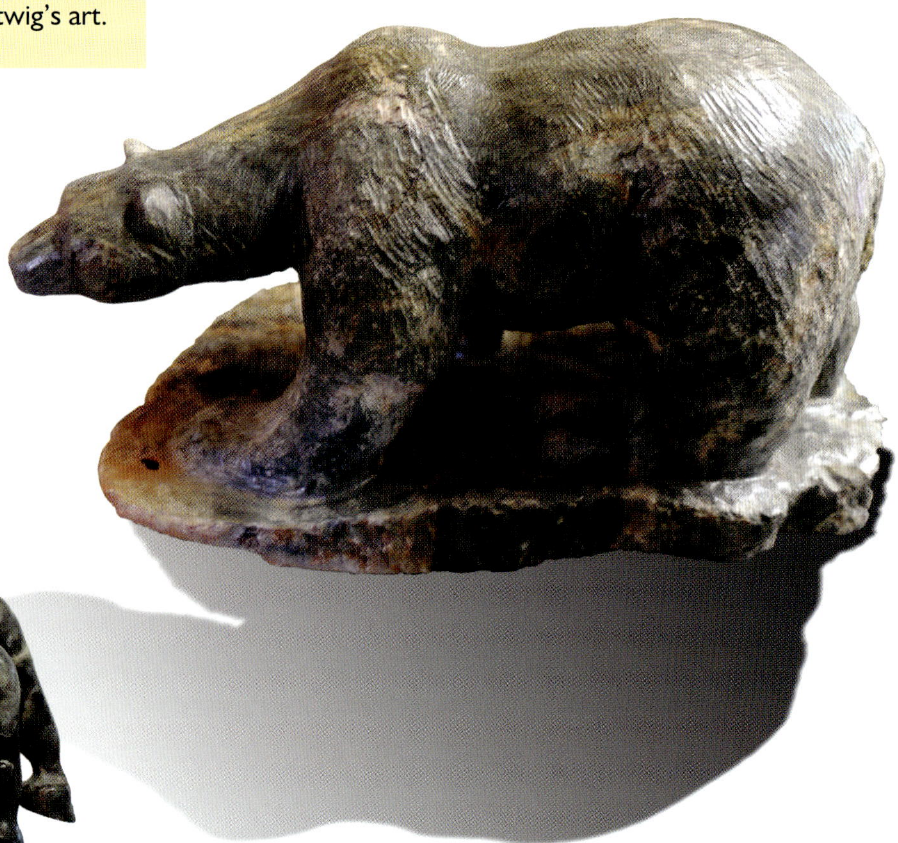

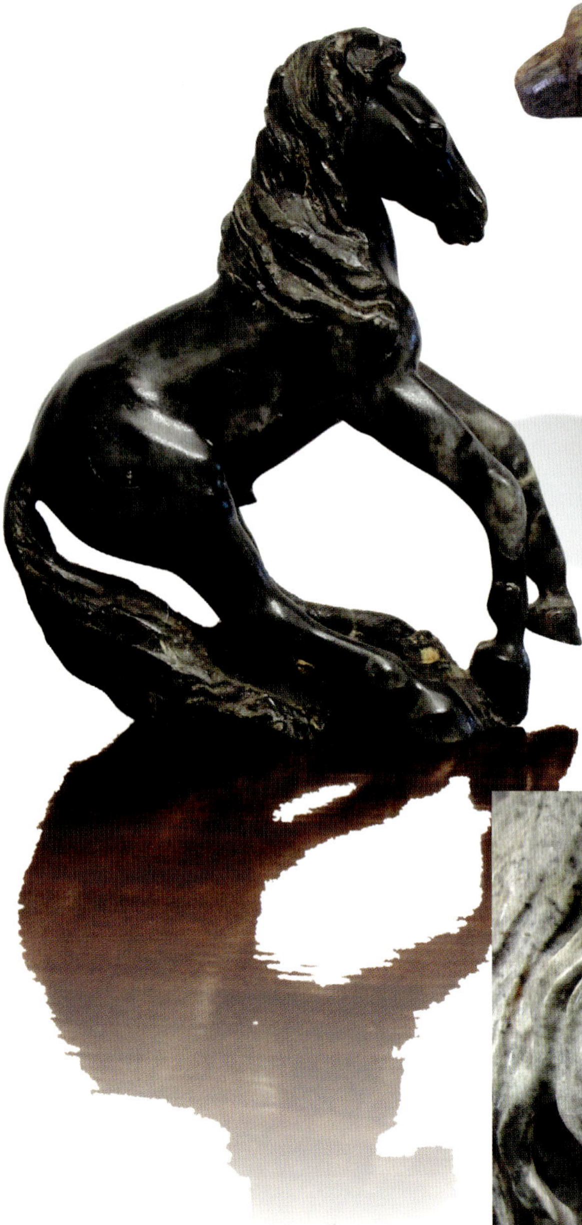

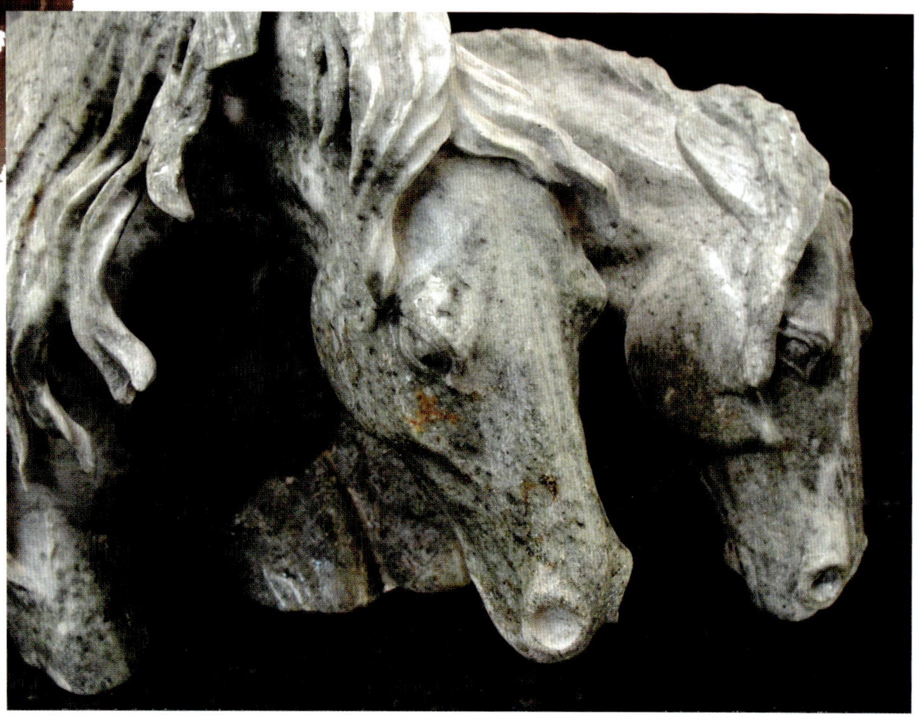